D1002929

TAMAR'S REVENGE

Tirso de Molina

TAMAR'S REVENGE

English version by James Fenton
after a literal translation by Simon Masterson

OBERON BOOKS

LONDON

The Royal Shakespeare Company

The Royal Shakespeare Company is one of the world's best known theatre ensembles, which aims to create outstanding theatre relevant to our times. The RSC is at the leading edge of classical theatre, with an international reputation for artistic excellence, accessibility and high quality live performance.

The Spanish Golden Age celebrates one of the most dynamic, energetic and stylish periods of world drama that is, astonishingly, hardly known to any of us. The four neglected plays from 17th century Spain which the RSC chose to present dramatised our fascination with the themes of seduction, honour and revenge.

The season was unique in a number of ways. It was the first time that an ensemble of British actors had come together over a period of time to bring these plays to life. It is also a new venture for the RSC and importantly for many of our audience who will not have had the opportunity to see the plays before.

The RSC performs throughout the year at our home in Stratford-upon-Avon and that work is complemented by a presence in other areas of the UK. We play regularly in London and at an annual residency in Newcastle upon Tyne. In addition, our mobile auditorium tour sets up in community centres, sports halls and schools in areas throughout the UK with little access to professional theatre.

While the UK is the home of our Company, our audiences are global. We regularly play to theatregoers in other parts of Europe, across the United States, the Americas, Asia and Australasia and we are proud of our relationships with partnering organisations throughout the world.

The RSC is at heart an ensemble Company. The continuation of this great tradition informs the work of all members of the Company. Directors, actors, dramatists and theatre practitioners all collaborate in the creation of the RSC's distinctive and unmistakable approach to theatre.

 # The Royal Shakespeare Company

Patron
Her Majesty The Queen
President
His Royal Highness The Prince of Wales
Deputy President
Sir Geoffrey Cass MA CIMgt

Artistic Director
Michael Boyd
Executive Director
Vikki Heywood

Board
Lord Alexander of Weedon QC *(Chairman)*
Sir Christopher Bland *(Chairman Elect)*
Lady Sainsbury of Turville *(Deputy Chairman)*
Lady Anderson
Jonathan Bate
Neil W Benson FCA
Ms Sinead Cusack
Jane Drabble
Mrs Janet M Gaymer
Mrs Sarah Harrity MBE
Michael Hoffman
Laurence Isaacson
Nicholas Lovegrove
Dana G Mead
Andrew Seth
A K Wilson MA

The Royal Shakespeare Company is incorporated under Royal Charter and is a registered charity, number 212481.

A PARTNERSHIP WITH THE RSC

The RSC relies on the active involvement and the direct charitable support of our audience members for contributions towards our work. Members of our audience also assist by introducing us to companies, foundations and other organisations with which they have an involvement – and help us demonstrate that in return for either philanthropic or sponsorship support, we can deliver benefit to audiences, local communities, school groups and all those who are given enhanced access to our work through private sector support.

RSC PATRONS AND SHAKESPEARE'S CIRCLE

Personal contributions from RSC Patrons provide essential financial support for our artists, educationalists and their students, young writers and audience members that require special access services.

For more information, please contact the Development Department on **01789 272283**.

CORPORATE PARTNERSHIPS

The RSC has a global reputation, undertaking more international touring each year than any other UK arts organisation. Our profile is high; our core values of artistic excellence and outstanding performance can be aligned with commercial values and objectives.

Our extensive range of productions and outreach and education programmes help ensure that we identify the best opportunity to deliver your particular business objectives. A prestigious programme of corporate hospitality and membership packages is also available.

For more information, please contact the Development Department on **01789 272283**.

For detailed information about opportunities to support the work of the RSC, visit **www.rsc.org.uk/support**

This production of *Tamar's Revenge* was first performed by
the Royal Shakespeare Company in the Swan Theatre,
Stratford-upon-Avon, on 28 April 2004.

The original cast was as follows:

William Buckhurst	Adonijah
James Chalmers	Absalom
Joseph Chance	Jonadab / Solomon
Julius D'silva	Braulio / Fencing Master
Rebecca Johnson	Abigail
Katherine Kelly	Tamar
Melanie MacHugh	Bathsheba / Shepherd
Vinta Morgan	Joab / Shepherd
Emma Pallant	Dina
Matt Ryan	Amnon
Peter Sproule	Tirso
John Stahl	David
Joanna Van Kampen	Laureta / Michal
John Wark	Ardelio
Oliver Williams	Eliazer / Shepherd

All other parts played by members of the Company

Directed by	Simon Usher
Designed by	Delia Peel
Season stage designed by	Es Devlin
Lighting designed by	Ben Ormerod
Music composed by	Neil McArthur
Sound designed by	Mike Compton
Movement by	Gaby Agis
Fights directed by	James Chalmers
Assistant Director	Chris White
Music Director	Michael Tubbs
Voice and dialect work by	Jeannette Nelson
Casting Director	John Cannon CDG
Production Manager	Pete Griffin
Costume Supervisor	Susie Duffy

Company Manager	Jondon
Stage Manager	Paul Sawtell
Deputy Stage Manager	Gabrielle Sanders
Assistant Stage Manager	Ruth Taylor

TAMAR'S REVENGE

First published in 2004 by Oberon Books Ltd.
(incorporating Absolute Classics)
521 Caledonian Road, London N7 9RH
Tel: 020 7607 3637 / Fax: 020 7607 3629

e-mail: oberon.books@btinternet.com
www.oberonbooks.com

Copyright © James Fenton 2004

James Fenton is hereby identified as author of this play in accordance
with section 77 of the Copyright, Designs and Patents Act 1988. The
author has asserted his moral rights.

All rights whatsoever in this play are strictly reserved and application for
performance etc. should be made before commencement of rehearsal to
PFD, Drury House, 34–43 Russell Street, London WC2B 5HA. No
performance may be given unless a licence has been obtained, and no
alterations may be made in the title or the text of the play without the
author's prior written consent.

This book is sold subject to the condition that it shall not by way of trade
or otherwise be circulated without the publisher's consent in any form of
binding or cover or circulated electronically other than that in which it is
published and without a similar condition including this condition being
imposed on any subsequent purchaser.

A catalogue record for this book is available from the British Library.

ISBN: 1 84002 442 9

Cover Design: Ann-marie Comarsh, RSC Graphics

Printed in Great Britain by Antony Rowe Ltd, Chippenham.

CHARACTERS

AMNON, A Crown Prince of Israel

ELIAZER, A Prince

JONADAB, A Prince

ABSALOM, A Prince

ADONIJAH

DINA

TAMAR

ABIGAIL, David's first wife

BATHSHEBA, One of David's wives

A SERVANT

JOSEPH, A bridegroom

ELISA, A bride

A FENCING-MASTER

JOAB

DAVID, The King

MICHAL, One of the David's wives

SOLOMON, A Prince

TIRSO, A shepherd

BRAULIO, A shepherd

ALISO, A shepherd

RISELO, A shepherd

ARDELIO, A shepherd

LAURETA, A seer

ACT ONE

Enter AMNON, dressed in travelling clothes, ELIAZER and JONADAB in Hebrew costume.

AMNON: Undo these spurs. Take off my boots.

ELIAZER: You must be tired of watching bastions fall
    And tired of scrambling over them.

AMNON: My father David's never tired.
    Even at his age he will not hear of peace.
    But when he was young, this sword of his
    Never so much as left his hand.

JONADAB: That's no surprise. When David was a boy
    He could cut off a giant's head, like that.
    And now he's old he'll find it difficult
    Coping with peace. It's hard to break old habits.

ELIAZER: Think of the way he won the crown,
    By his sheer bravery. That was how he rose.

AMNON: I can't compete with him. I am not such a soldier
    And I shall never have a fame like his.
    Let it be David –
    Let it be David who lays siege
    To the idol-worshipping Ammonites.
    Let him invent the ingenious machines
    To scale their bastions. That's what he loves to do.
    He loves to build his empire, Eliazer.
    But I – I should prefer a single hour,
    A single morning in Jerusalem
    To all of David's victories in the field
    And all the fame that he has won from them.

ELIAZER: Strange. If you were the afflicted lover,
    The suitor of some fine lady,
    I shouldn't wonder that you hated the war.
    Love's a pursuit for peacetime.
    War makes a lover impatient.

But if you are not in love – and still
Fighting disgusts you – well, that's something new.

AMNON: Yes, Eliazer, that is something new.
That's what I like about it – it's something new.
In everything I think, or, do, or feel,
I am unique. And what I value in others
Is their originality, the gift
To think of, to invent something that's new.

Enter ABSALOM, ADONIJAH and others, in travelling clothes.

ABSALOM: If we hadn't made it to Jerusalem
We'd have missed the celebrations for the truce.

ADONIJAH: Well we've come flying from Rabat to get here.

ABSALOM: Post-horses, Adonijah, were a great innovation.

ELIAZER: I curse the very thought of them.
These days of solid riding
Have given me a backside like grilled salmon.

ABSALOM: Eliazer!
Have you come to celebrate the truce as well?

ELIAZER: What do you think?

AMNON: Absalom, Adonijah, my brothers – you here?

ABSALOM: Time for some sowing of wild oats, brother.
There'll be no holding us. We're coming home,
Back to the palace after the tents of war.
Ten days of truce David has given the Ammonites,
Ten days for us, scaling the bastions of Love.

AMNON: The bastions of Love?

ABSALOM: A man goes out at night in search of love.
Are there not bastions to assault?
Streets to patrol, windows to penetrate,
Passwords to whisper, stratagems to devise.
That proves it: Eros and Mars are as one.

AMNON: I'll not dispute it. Eros is the son of Mars,
Love in its way takes after War.

It's a short step from one thing to the other.

ABSALOM: In your case, Prince, it's an infinity.
    Great soldier, man that you are,
    I think that you have never been in love.

AMNON: I do not fan the flames of love, like you do.
    I'm not as smooth a talker as you are,
    My brother Absalom.

ABSALOM: Beauty is a manifestation of perfection
    And what is perfect is designed for love.
    My fate has made me beautiful, and I
    Prefer to share it around in any way I can.

AMNON: Your hair has made you beautiful
    And that is why you get away with anything.
    You pitch your tent, the girls come crowding round
    And they're begging for it, begging you to sell
    One of your locks. They say that every hair
    Is paid for, direct, with interest. And they say
    You've had a girl for every single hair on your head.

ELIAZER: And this hair of yours, it covers up their defects.
    No wonder they adore you. All Jerusalem
    Calls you the bald girl's friend. They swear by you,
    And use you as a tonic or a beauty aid.
    And there are all those children running around
    With little Absalom heads – thousands of them.

ABSALOM: Eliazer, these subjects are unworthy.

ELIAZER: No. Without you the prettiest of our girls
    Would be as bald as garlic.

ABSALOM: So, Prince, your plan
    Is to go without the love of a good woman.

AMNON: Until I meet perfection in a woman,
    Love will not find me on his list.

ABSALOM: Elizabeth is beautiful enough.

AMNON: Look closer, brother, she's pock-marked and rough.

ADONIJAH: Esther –

AMNON: has the complexion, but her teeth are bad.

ELIAZER: Delbora –

AMNON: Big mouth –

JONADAB: Athalia?

AMNON: She's mad,
    And stunted with it.

ABSALOM: Maria? What's wrong there?

AMNON: The constant simpering is too much to bear.

ADONIJAH: Dina?

AMNON: She's a foot taller than one could wish.

ELIAZER: Ruth?

AMNON: Ruth is black.

JONADAB: Rachel?

AMNON: Cold as a fish.

ABSALOM: Aristobola?

AMNON: Everyone knows about her.
    She promises herself to a hundred men a year.

ABSALOM: Judith?

ABSALOM: Has blotchy skin and smells of tar.

ADONIJAH: Martha?

ABSALOM: Has acne.

ELIAZER: Alexandra?

AMNON: Is a har-

JONADAB: Jezebel?

AMNON: They say her hands are covered with warts.

ABSALOM: Silene?

AMNON: A pretty face. Says more than she ought.

16

ELIAZER: Well, if you can't find any girl to love,
    You can always make yourself one out of clay.

ABSALOM: For God's sake, brother – you're satirical **tod**ay.

AMNON: No, you will never see this prince in love.
    I have a malign condition that prevents me.

ADONIJAH: That means you won't be wanting to come with us
    To the wedding-party the young people of the court
    Are giving for Elisa.

AMNON: Who's she marrying?

ADONIJAH: Didn't you know? Joseph of Isacar.

AMNON: A man like him deserves a beautiful wife.

ABSALOM: She won't impress you. You never fall in love.
    Will you be going?

AMNON: Me? I'm not so sure.

ADONIJAH: The party will be spectacular.

AMNON: I'll go,
    But only for the dancing, not to ogle her.
    I shall disguise myself. Are masks allowed?

ADONIJAH: At these receptions, yes.

AMNON: My heart goes out to the groom – stuck, with a wife.

ELIAZER: You're not much like your father in that respect.

AMNON: You never tire of that subject, do you?
    I am aware, of course, that David, my father,
    Is not averse to other people's wives: There's Abigail, Nabal's
        wife, and Bathsheba,
    The beautiful mother of smiling Solomon.

ADONIJAH: And all the concubines, and all their beauty –
    A miracle on earth, or so they say.
    I've always wanted to get a look at them.

AMNON: But David keeps them under lock and key
    And Death himself would be hard put to get in there.

17

ABSALOM: What with the over-security of the palace,
  And the gross unreliability of women,
  It can be hard to spend any time with them.
  The other day I saw one of the younger ones
  And, by God, Amnon, she stole my soul away.

AMNON: Adonijah, come, listen to Absalom.
  You are in love with one of your father's wives.

ABSALOM: My father has wives and concubines to spare.
  The only one *I* would spare is my own mother.
  That's how it is with me. Whenever David marries,
  I fall in love again out of pure envy.
  I'm envious of the old lecher, Amnon,
  And there will come a time, I tell you,
  When I've enjoyed all his wives, the lot of them.

AMNON: Beauty and madness are sisters.
  You are beautiful, and you are mad.

ADONIJAH: Your fortune is in your hair – and that is all.
  Don't go talking nonsense.
  It's getting dark. What is your plan tonight?

ABSALOM: There is a certain lady I must visit
  As soon as her all neighbours are asleep.

ADONIJAH: I'm dying for a game of cards.

AMNON: Well, I am not in love, and I don't gamble.
  I shall go and read some poetry.

ABSALOM: Very restful.

AMNON: Yes, and in this I emulate my father
  Since I could never match him in desire.

ABSALOM: You will become a poet, and a saint.

ADONIJAH: As David has his psalms, God is his muse
  And he will inspire our brother too.

ABSALOM: He will become a poet and a prophet
  And penetrate inexpressible mysteries.

AMNON: You are both very spiritual.

ABSALOM: Yes, but we are going off to humanise ourselves.
  Do you want to come with us?

AMNON: No, brothers, goodbye.

ALL: Goodbye.

  Exit ABSALOM and ADONIJAH.

ELIAZER: What shall we do now?

AMNON: I don't know what has got into me today.
  I have a kind of craving.

ELIAZER: You're pregnant.

AMNON: Think of those women, locked in the palace
  And my father off in the field, and anyway
  Too old for love. What can they do all day?
  It's a known fact,
  A woman is the mirror of her husband's honour,
  And yet when it comes to fidelity and reputation
  A woman's fragile, an imperfect creature.

JONADAB: Privation is the mother of appetite...
  A man is the completion of a woman...
  Your father's away... Women are fickle...

ELIAZER: They spend all their time dreaming...
  Anything for pleasure...

AMNON: You are a fine pair of philosophers.

ELIAZER: I'm just sorry for them, for heaven's sake,
  The ladies of the palace, locked up in a casket.

AMNON: The weather is close. What with the night and the cloud
  It's dark in there, and I would guess the ladies
  Would be out walking now, in the cool of the garden
  Looking for relief. And I've an appetite
  Which I must do something to satisfy.
  I feel a curiosity.

ELIAZER: What will you do?

AMNON: Me?

   I shall jump over the wall, get into the park,
   See how the women entertain themselves.

ELIAZER: I wouldn't risk it.
   If the king heard of it, he'd be enraged.
   You know anyone caught in there, however noble,
   Would be killed at once. The king's house is a sanctuary,
   Just like a temple.

AMNON: That is true. But the Crown Prince
   Is above the law. I am the Prince of Israel,
   The heat here is abominably cruel
   And this is how I choose to distract myself.
   You know how, when I get an idea, sometimes
   I have to follow it through.

JONADAB: Then come, start climbing.
   But it seems dangerous and quite pointless to me.

AMNON: The point is: my satisfaction of my desires.

JONADAB: And after you have gratified your whim?

AMNON: If I have said it will be so, by God, it will be.
   Let's go and find how to get in.

ELIAZER: Get in? Who?

AMNON: Me, while you two wait outside.

ELIAZER: Wait a moment.

AMNON: I saw some ivy growing there
   Clinging so tightly to the stone,
   I could use that.

ELIAZER: Go on then, and start climbing.
   Whenever he gets a notion in his head
   Fourteen preachers couldn't talk him out of it.

JONADAB: Our masters are a strange breed.

ELIAZER: And this one of ours – how's that for recklessness?

 Exeunt.

 Enter DINA, with a guitar, and TAMAR.

TAMAR: Have you ever known such heat?
Of course it's easier for you than it is for me.

DINA: Easier?

TAMAR: For you,
The night is hot, but not with the fires of love.
I cannot breathe. I cannot bear a moment more.
I am suffocating, choking from love and heat.
What will become of me?

DINA: You will turn into an oven
And in that oven you will bake a loaf
That loaf you bake will be a tender thought.
You will give that bread to your beloved Joab
To feed him against the violent pangs of jealousy.

TAMAR: Yes,
When we make bold to open our hearts to him,
Love pays us back with jealousy.

DINA: It is remarkably calm. Not a single leaf
Stirs in the lazy wind.

TAMAR: But here's a river that defies the heat.
And here the golden cup of sand
Contains a meadow. Let us sit down on the bank.

DINA: Hundreds and hundreds of flowers,
Like cushions of brocade
Offer a royal throne,
A throne for a princess.

TAMAR: You have your instrument. Sing.
That's how the god of Love is soothed
In beautiful gardens.

DINA: I'm not in love. I have no ills to soothe.
But you could summon up a gentle breeze
For you are famed for music as for beauty
And, hearing you, the zephyr will run out,
Happy to do you service at your song.

TAMAR: You flatter me.

DINA: No,
But if you sing I shall have a chance to rest.

Enter AMNON, without being seen by them.

AMNON: ~~I'm young. I don't ask~~ why I do what I do.
I follow my desires, and the night protects me.
There is the darkness and it makes me sad,
But this bright river in the moonlight gives me joy.
Because I do not know where I am going
I stumble over everything I come to.

TAMAR: Dina, I am very sad.

DINA: I find that singing gives a kind of truce
To grief.

TAMAR: Give me that instrument, then.

AMNON: My wish is granted. I can hear women's voices.

TAMAR: Music was made to ease the suffering spirit.

AMNON: I came at the right moment. They are about to sing.

TAMAR: If only my love could hear me.

AMNON: Nowhere is safe from the assaults of Love.
His influence reaches even here.

TAMAR sings.

TAMAR: *Heavy my heart at nightfall,*
Light are the thoughts of love –
Green are the wings of the bird of hope,
Soft as the voice of a dove.
And the green wings are beating –
I can hear them fall from the sky
Down to the evening river
To the cool of the waterside.

Drink, drink from the river,
By the medlar tree.
Drink from the evening waters.
Green bird, come back to me.

What if my love has left me?
What if my fears are true?
Take him a message in your beak.
Make him listen to you.
Punish him for his silence.
But if he's thinking of me
Promise him I've a gift for him
Under the medlar tree.

Drink, drink from the river
By the medlar tree.
Drink from the evening waters.
Green bird, come back to me.

AMNON: Listen to that lovely voice
    And the burning cries of sorrow,
    Subtle mastery of art –
    Listen as the spell is cast.
    Now the wind is picking up
    As if ashamed at ever stopping
    And a harmony begins
    With the trebles of the leaves
    And the bass voice of the river.
    Love, I know not what to say
    For it seems that your dominion
    Comes by night, comes like a thief
    And can make a lover blind.
    A woman can have an angel's voice
    And the features of a serpent.
    But what if her face is as her voice?
    Then you will have had your way,
    You will have won, almighty boy,
    Over this rebellious heart,
    Made this noble heart your subject –
    Made me a slave, and made me love.

DINA: Sing again. Call up the sun
    For he is a famed musician.
    He will come and hear you sing.
    He will come to see your beauty.

AMNON: Let it come and let it shine.
Who could doubt that she is fair?
Who could wonder if her face
Is the reflection of her song.
Make me worthy now to see
What my ears have heard this night.

TAMAR: Why should I sing?
Why should I sing in sorrow?

AMNON: Welcome, cruel jealousy,
Come to teach my heart a lesson
In the ways of newborn love.
And this woman is apart
Yet she is faithful to her lover
And I have stepped into the prison
Into the chains of cruel love,
Fallen in love before I've seen her,
Taken prisoner in a day.
Strong is Eros, blind though he be.

DINA: Let your love be like your song
And your love be like a springtime
Stretching for a thousand years.
Sing again. You have amazed
The evening heat and it grows gentler
As it stops to listen to you.

TAMAR sings.

TAMAR: *My love's by the evening river*
And my thoughts linger with him.
Come back to me, come back to me
Now that the trees are dim.
But my thoughts are with my lover.
They are at his fingertips
And they laugh at me, at my jealousy
As they drink from his lips.

Drink, drink from the river
By the medlar tree.
Drink from the evening waters,
Green bird, come back to me.

AMNON: Could peace be more complete? Celestial Spirits,
If you should wish to see your portrait painted
By mortal music, come with me. Come closer.
But I fall.

He trips and falls.

TAMAR: Oh heavens. Who is here?

AMNON: I cannot hide
But in this night I can conceal my identity.
It is so dark, for sure, no one will look
Closely enough to recognise my clothes.

TAMAR: Who is that?

AMNON: Give me a hand, my lady. I'm the gardener's son. I fell over, what with listening to that music, I tripped on a log and banged my shin. Can't you see me?

DINA: You can't see where you're walking, and you expect us to see you?

AMNON: You sing prettily enough, whoever you are. I could sit and listen to you for a fortnight without a wink of sleep.

TAMAR: You liked what you heard.

AMNON: By God you sang like a giant, like a Goliath. Your hand, lady, I'm as heavy as a hill. (*Aside.*)

I took her hand and kissed it too.
Honey was never sweeter.

TAMAR: You are too bold.

AMNON: What do you expect? Nothing venture nothing gain.

TAMAR: So you are the gardener?

AMNON: I am the gardener, and an aficionado of a little night music.

DINA: Quite the jester.

AMNON: You sing well, and, if fortune has given you as much help in the face as in the voice, you must be a rare beauty. But they say a fair face and fair voice seldom go together.

TAMAR: That's a crude thought.

25

AMNON: It's what they often say when a woman sings well: 'Better you were heard but not seen.' It's shocking but it's true.

TAMAR: That wish of yours is granted by this darkness.

AMNON: It's frustrating, hearing you and not seeing you.

TAMAR: So you don't know me.

AMNON: There are so many of you coming here to the garden, day and night. Even if you were one of the ones who come to me for a bit of a good time – for the King is old now, and can hardly do justice to all of you – I'd still have my work cut out to recognise you. There are so many of you, I'm always getting pinched somewhere.

TAMAR: What a scoundrel.

DINA: Vicious gossip.

TAMAR: People like him are always having a go at us.

AMNON: If you tell me who you are, madam, I shall bring you some flowers and fruit.

TAMAR: You talk too much.

AMNON removes one of her gloves.

AMNON: (*Aside.*) I got one of her gloves when I went to kiss her hand.

TAMAR: Come, Dina, let us go.

AMNON: Don't go. Sing. Maybe Heaven will reward you by making David young again, if he is your husband.

TAMAR: I have dropped a glove.

AMNON: It must be on the ground. I've found it. Not doing badly at finding things tonight.

TAMAR: Where is it?

AMNON: Take it.

TAMAR: Give it to me.

AMNON kisses her hand.

AMNON: I have kissed her hand again.

TAMAR: Who gave you leave to be so bold?

AMNON: Only my good fortune.

TAMAR: Give the glove here.

AMNON: Fooled you.

He goes to hand it to her but snatches it back again.

TAMAR: Then you didn't find it.

AMNON: No.

TAMAR: How do you like that?

DINA: Quite a gardener.

AMNON: (*Aside.*) In the garden of love.
    It's not all flowers here.

TAMAR: I shall have you thrown out. Come, Dina.

DINA: Are you going to Elisa's wedding tomorrow?

TAMAR: Yes.

DINA: Which dress?

TAMAR: The scarlet.

AMNON: You will be a crimson carnation, and I shall try my
    luck elsewhere. Are you leaving without any more singing?
    Won't you tell me your names before you go?

DINA: Why should we tell our names to a scoundrel?

Exeunt TAMAR and DINA.

AMNON: Now it is true. I really am in darkness
    For till this day I had the sun before me.
    I came here free from love. I used to laugh at it.
    Now I could weep for it.

Weep for the lovely voice, the tangled darkness,
Weep in the hope that the face is like the music,
Pray that this glove will be augur of good fortune
Now that I need it.

I who was carefree – now to be defeated,
Lead the assault, and find myself the victim,

To be in love, but not to known my loved one,
Me, to be caught like this!

Fate, let me learn who she is, my new tormentor,
Learn from the dress she chooses for tomorrow.
The die is cast. Let me not choose the blank lot.
Let me choose the red lot.

Exit AMNON. Enter ABSALOM, ADONIJAH, ABIGAIL (the Queen) and BATHSHEBA.

ABIGAIL: Was the King well when you left him?

ABSALOM: Happy and in health.
He seems to grow young on war. Fury renews him
And valour makes him ever more vigorous.

ABIGAIL: He will forget his wives, with all these victories.

ADONIJAH: His love for you is his trophy,
Your conversation is reward enough for him.

ABSALOM: David has given you little cause to fear
He might forget you. At least, I do not know
There ever was a truer lover in wartime
Nor a finer soldier in times of peace.
Believe me – his mind is always on you
Even when his sword is at his enemy's throat.

ADONIJAH: Bathsheba knows this well, and Abigail
Needs no reminding.

ABIGAIL: All that I know is that I am sad without him.

BATHSHEBA: And I – I come alive whenever I see him
And weep when he is not here.

ABIGAIL: Are you returning to the siege so soon?

ADONIJAH: The truce he has agreed is very brief.
There's little time.

ABSALOM: I shall be going tomorrow.

ADONIJAH: Me too.

ABIGAIL: Well, I shall send a letter with you

Telling the King that if he really loves me
He will return to safety in Jerusalem
And not exhaust his silvered head at war.
Maybe to say so is to question his strength
But still a man is wise, when he is old,
To hang his sword up, and to learn
To fight his battles with the pen instead.

ABSALOM: My father is skilled in either art.

BATHSHEBA: You are looking handsome tonight, Absalom.

ABSALOM: It's for the wedding.

BATHSHEBA: And you, Prince, are out to seduce the court.

ADONIJAH: We're guests of honour at the party.
　　We know the bride.

Enter AMNON, dejected, with JONADAB and ELIAZER.

ELIAZER: What's happened?

AMNON: I have exchanged
　　My life for someone else's.

JONADAB: Ever since you ventured in that garden,
　　You've been like this, not sleeping and not yourself.
　　What happened to you there?

ELIAZER: What did you see?

AMNON: I grieve because of what I did not see.
　　I am trying to change my philosophy and my life
　　And conversation is no use to me.
　　The only thing that understands me now
　　Is my imagination. Leave me alone with it.

Aside.

　　If I could see that scarlet dress.
　　If it were just to pass before me now.

ABSALOM: Prince.

ABIGAIL: Amnon, my dear.

AMNON: This truce has given us the chance to see you.

29

ADONIJAH: And now Elisa's wedding
  Has brought a further celebration.

AMNON: She is worthy of the honour.

ABSALOM: For you these occasions are only fit to be mocked.

AMNON: I don't know what you mean.

 Enter a SERVANT.

SERVANT: My lords, Joseph hopes you will honour him with your
  company.

ADONIJAH: We are obliged.

ABSALOM: Are you coming, prince?

AMNON: Shortly. But I have something else to do.

ABSALOM: Let's go then, Adonijah.

 Exeunt all but AMNON.

AMNON: Rise now, my scarlet dawn, and let me fall
  Prostrate before your feet. When your sun's light
  Illuminates my day, and when your voice
  Enraptures like the harmony of heaven,
  Then I shall know you. Then I shall know your face
  Is equal to the melody I heard.
  But what if she were simply to change her mind?
  What if some whim should lead her not to wear
  The colour that is to be my go-between?
  What if the god of love should take his revenge
  And punish me for my too free behaviour?
  Let it not be so, Eros. O my blindfolded god,
  I am aflame. Let me find out today
  Who is the woman. Who has set this fire?
  Pay no attention to my arrogance
  For I surrender up my arms to you.
  Here come the newly-weds, and the court with them.

*Music sounds, and the whole company enters in pairs, dressed in
all their finery. TAMAR wears a sumptuous scarlet dress; the
newly-weds enter last of all. They process once around the stage
and exit.*

Now I breathe in happy doubt.
Now I brood in loving fear.
Many and various are the ways
Eros sets a heart ablaze.
Hidden here, I wait to see
Who my tyrant love shall be.

O God, a crimson dress
That burns me like a flame.
No, what is this? Is this the lot I have drawn?
Isn't this Tamar in the scarlet dress –
Tamar, my sister. I am mad. I'm in love –
My mind runs wild and finds no place to rest.
I'm in love with my sister Tamar.
It was a dark night. I came home to Jerusalem.
I curse that night. I curse my own madness.
I came home of my own free will, I climbed the wall
Of my own free will. I was mad.
I climbed the wall of love, of tyrannous love.
Brother and lover, I am a brother and lover.
Oh, I had rather let this fire die in my breast –
Let it die. I shall go back to the war,
Back to the siege and let my passion die,
Before it has the chance to grow stronger than me.

Enter ELIAZER and JONADAB

Eliazer.

ELIAZER: My lord.

AMNON: Go and fetch…

ELIAZER: What is it?

AMNON: I want to dress for the road and go back to the field.
Get me my boots and spurs.

JONADAB: I shall go see to the post-horses.

AMNON: But how can the hawk fly when it is blind in its hood?
Forget that.
Bring me a costume and a mask to wear.

I want to join the party.

Exeunt ELIAZER and JONADAB.

I am a monster of impossibility
And in my hope is my despair.
The dolphin loved Arion.
Xerxes fell in love with a plane tree
And another man was obsessed by a statue.
And Semiramis, the great Assyrian queen,
Fell in love with a wild beast.
My madness makes my torment worse.
I fell in love with a voice.
I love my own sister.

Enter ELIAZER and JONADAB.

JONADAB: Here is the costume and the mask.

AMNON: Dress me, then. No, let me be.
I must restrain myself, but the need hounds me
And I'm losing my composure and my reason.
Leave me alone. Will you not go?

ELIAZER: (*Aside.*) What has possessed him?

Exeunt ELIAZER and JONADAB.

AMNON: If this is love there was not long to wait
Nor far to go before I tasted Hell.
I am a Prince of Israel. God forbid
One cruel urge like this should bring me down.
I am a Prince of Israel, and it is noble –
A noble thing to die.
I am a Prince and a slave of a blind god.
Love and be silent? No one can do it.

*Exit AMNON. Enter all the wedding party, among them TAMAR.
They sit.*

TAMAR: Joseph and Elisa,
Enjoy your lives together
And let old age reward you
With fair and noble children,

    The fruits of the autumn,
    The harvest of your love.

JOSEPH: If your Highness wishes
    All the things you promise,
    Who can doubt our fortune?

ELISA: Or that we shall try our
    Utmost to repay you
    The great debt we owe you.

Enter a SERVANT.

SERVANT: They are calling for a masked dance.

TAMAR: Let the festivities begin.

They sit. Enter AMNON, masked. Dancing.

JOSEPH: Look at Tamar now.
    There's a true beauty and a matchless grace.

AMNON kneels beside TAMAR, still masked.

AMNON: Now, Eros, what's the use of any resistance?
    You pull at me so violently that I
    Am dragged along behind. My tyrant, my love
    Stands unaccompanied and impossible.
    Thank you for that at least. My cruel sister,
    What a barrier heaven has placed before our love.

To TAMAR.

    Madam, if it could always be like this,
    I'd see a woman wed every hour of the day.
    And in the dark night too – that's a fine place for unions.
    In the dark of the night, a garden can become a bridal chamber.
    A garden like yours, for instance,
    When the weather is stifling,
    And the song of a seraph… heaven in a voice!
    I know who it was
    Who heard your voice and fell in love with you last night.
    I know who it was
    Who kissed a hand and kissed it again. I know…

TAMAR: I understand what you are saying.
    You played a malicious trick.
    You pretended to be a gardener
    And you desecrated the sanctity of the palace.
    Just be grateful I do not intend
    To spoil this party. If I were to act,
    I would make you a warning to others.
    That garden would be the scene of your punishment.

AMNON: My scene of punishment – yes.
    It is already the scene of my punishment.
    And I wish I could warn myself against myself.
    But I have no fear of punishment.
    Heaven has stripped me of fear.
    I myself feed the fires that burn me.

TAMAR: Who are you to talk to me like this?

AMNON: I am a thing composed of opposites
    Which, from the time I first encountered you
    Have been tormenting me: a monstrous chimaera,
    A sphinx with which I wrestle inside myself,
    Paradoxical, a volcano of freezing snow.
    It comes to this, Princess. The longer I am with you
    The more I shrink towards nothingness.

TAMAR: You are completely mad.

AMNON: I know what you lost last night. I gained a glove.
    You gave your hand to a peasant. Give it now
    To a noble suitor.

TAMAR: Your mask has lost its comedy.
    Leave here at once or I shall have you killed.

AMNON: I lost my life last night.
    Whoever seeks it now will be too late.
    You show more favour to a peasant by night
    Than to a courtier. I shall kiss your hand
    Whether you like it or not.

He kisses her hand and exits.

TAMAR: You there. Kill that man.

All rise, concerned and puzzled.

Forget the party. Go after him.

JOSEPH: What's the matter? What has upset you?

TAMAR: Do not ask.
Kill that man or I shall be accursed.

ELISA: The party is over. Do what Her Highness says.

JOSEPH: The greatest pleasures end in grief.

End of Act One

ACT TWO

Enter AMNON in a melancholy mood. He is dressing, and brings with him clothes and a hunting cap. Also ELIAZER and JONADAB.

JONADAB: You are not right, sir, to get up so soon.

AMNON: Bed is torture, like the rack.

ELIAZER: A wise man has compared it to jealousy.

AMNON: In what way?

ELIAZER: Both can be good for you in moderation.
    Too much can cause weakness, or death.

AMNON: Well said. You there!

JONADAB: Sir.

AMNON: Give him a hundred escudos.

ELIAZER: You pay like a prince, for works, and for words.

AMNON goes to wash his hands in a bowl of water.

AMNON: What is this?

JONADAB: Water for your hands.

AMNON: Better to wash with fire, since water scalds me.
    Tell me something amusing.
    Why don't you say something, Eliazer?

ELIAZER: I don't know how to please you.
    One moment you are calling at the top of your voice
    For people to distract you with stories,
    Next you want music,
    Then you dismiss the story-tellers
    And start shouting at the singers.

JONADAB: This melancholy of yours
    Is worrying all Jerusalem.

ELIAZER: There is nobody – man or woman –

Who would not be prepared to buy back your health
With some part of their own.

AMNON: So, do they love me?

JONADAB: They love you as they ought to love their prince.

AMNON: Enough. Don't talk to me of women.
If only there were a way to conserve the race
Without the need for women. Where's the doctor?

JONADAB: You ordered that no doctor should visit you.

AMNON: If they knew what they were talking about half the time,
I'd be a healthy man.

ELIAZER: They don't study words.
Bleeding and purging is what they know about.

AMNON: What do they earn?

JONADAB: It's all silk, amber, mules.
If, instead of getting up an army,
David sent two doctors against Syria,
The thought of the bill would cause an instant surrender.

ELIAZER: Delbora's been ill for days, and there were six doctors
at her house yesterday, consulting as to the best treatment.
They withdrew to the next room, throwing out its occupants,
and a maid decided to listen at the door. The first doctor was
saying: 'My dear friend, what would you reckon to make in a
fortnight?' 'Fifty escudos,' says the other: 'I've bought a farm,
twenty acres of vineyard, a meadow... But I must say, you've
got some property yourself – very tasteful.' 'Yes,' says the first,
'I hardly know what to do with my earnings. Funny, isn't it –
we're not executioners, but we get paid for killing people.' A
third man says, 'How was the game last night?' 'The dice were
against me. Do you play?' 'Play?' says this doctor. 'My idea of
play, since you ask, is a fourteen-year-old girl I visited the
other day, who'd had a fainting fit. I found her alone and in
bed. I felt her pulse, then I palpated her breasts, and – you
know what it's like as soon as there's touching – a certain
appetite is aroused. I explained certain things to her, then gave
a demonstration of what I meant. And now she's plump and in

the pink of health. She appreciates my figure, my taste, my conversation – even my scent. So now she's ill all over again, for love of me.' 'You seem to have enjoyed her.' 'Let's say we've watched the sunrise together. It's an odd profession, ours. No door is locked to us, no opportunity barred. The coyest woman in the world, who dithers for years before rewarding her love-sick suitor with the faintest glimpse of her face, surrenders the bed to us, at the first sally. Young, naked, loving every minute of it – they seem to make a special exception for us. We do the job. We get all the respect, and there's a nice profit too.' 'If I were the King,' says another, ' I'd only allow eunuchs to treat the sick – or women for women, men for men.' 'If you did that,' says the first, 'I'd quit the job. There's no pay can match the right to look after young girls and married women.' 'Got many books?' says one. 'Books? I've got two hundred of 'em, all covered in dust. They never say anything to me, and I never give 'em a glance. That's how we get on. We doctors earn our keep through two things: ostentation and ignorance. It's been more than a fortnight since I consulted anything that wasn't white turkey breast, loin of rabbit in pepper and orange sauce, partridge, pigeon and veal. C'mon. That's enough deliberation. Let's visit the patient and pronounce.' So they went next door, and the one with the longest beard said: 'Massage the legs, fourteen cups on the back, three or four incisions, saffron and orange-blossom poultice on the heart – and she'll be as right as rain.' And they went off with two hundred reales in the purse.

AMNON: Silence, you fool, your talk torments me.
    What on earth makes you talk so much?

ELIAZER: Sir, you commanded me.
    If I am silent, you take offence,
    And if I talk you threaten me.

AMNON: What's that? Who's singing?

JONADAB: The musicians you called for, to sing you out of your
    mood.

AMNON: A waste of effort.

Singing within.

MUSICIANS: *Happy happy little sparrows,*
Singing at the break of day
Tirralee, tirralay,
Do not, do not fly away –
Happy, ha-a-ppee-ee leetle sparrows
Do not, do not fly away.

Sing a song to drown his sorrows,
Sing a song to make him gay,
Tirralee, tirralay -
Sing a song to make him gay
Happy ha-a-ppee-ee leetle sparrows
Do not, do not fly away.

The third verse imitates bird-song. AMNON interrupts.

AMNON: Eliazer, Jonadab, throw them out of the window.
Put them to death.
Bury them with their stupid instruments.

JONADAB: This is a strange passion of melancholy.

AMNON: A servant should imitate his master in his home.
Why should they be singing?
Does my illness please them?

Enter a FENCING-MASTER.

ELIAZER: Here is the fencing-master for your lesson.

AMNON: Give me the black foil, though the white steel tempts
me.
My hope was never green. Now it is washed away.

FENCING-MASTER: My Lord, may Heaven put colour in your
face
For it is withered in sadness and want of health.

AMNON: Impertinent speech-maker,
The true fighter never talks.
Come. Wield your arms in silence.

FENCING-MASTER: Forgive me my lord,
In the last lesson I showed you

That with these two figures – so… and so –
A man can gain half a foot on the enemy.

AMNON: Seven feet is what I want to gain, a body's length.
Oh, I shall have no peace till I have killed you.

Goes after him.

FENCING-MASTER: What is your lordship doing?

AMNON: Punishing your arrogance.
You fools, the sickness that's afflicting me
Is born of love. Weapons will not extract it.
Die, all of you, die. I am set upon
By invisible enemies.

FENCING-MASTER: Let's go till his rage is calmed.

They all flee.

AMNON: If there were weapons could kill my memories,
They would be weapons indeed. Eliazer, Jonadab!
Joseph, Abiatar, Sisara!
Someone do something about the torment that burns me.

Enter ELIAZER and JONADAB.

JONADAB: My Lord, be calm.

AMNON: How can I be calm if my soul is a chimera,
A monstrous union of a lion, a snake and a goat?
I am a paradox, a thing of contradictions.
A moment ago I was lying here in bed –
Who has put all this finery on me?
Undress me, quickly, quickly.

ELIAZER: You dressed yourself.
You got up against all advice.

AMNON: Liar.

JONADAB: Shut up. Undress him.

AMNON: Why am I wearing silk? Why am I not in mourning?
My freedom is dead and I'm dressed for a celebration.
From this day forth I shall wear sackcloth, I shall wear black
In mourning for the liberty I have lost.

Drums sound within.

What's that?

JONADAB: Your father, sir. The King is coming,
    The monarch of the twelve illustrious tribes.
    The trumpets and the drums are sounding the triumph.
    David has overthrown the Ammonites
    And their idolatry in their rebel cities.
    Jerusalem now is going out to meet him
    To bring him home with music, hymns and dancing.
    They have adorned the gates with cedar and palm
    And all his grateful wives are setting forth
    To congratulate him. Surely the sight of his arrival
    Will make you forget your sorrow.

AMNON: When you are in the grip of melancholy,
    Other men's triumphs only make things worse.
    Leave my house. All of you. Leave me alone.
    Can you not see the company I keep –
    Madness, despair, sadness, paradox, rage?
    My father David has triumphed yet again.
    Now my distress will really finish me.

Exit AMNON.

JONADAB: He is to be pitied in his frenzy.

ELIAZER: And that he does not know the cause of it.

JONADAB: Love?

ELIAZER: If it were love, who is likely to refuse
    The heir to the throne of Israel?

JONADAB: By God I do not know. He will not speak of it.
    But Amnon is either in love or he is mad.

Enter to the sound of many fanfares JOAB, ABSALOM, ADONIJAH, marching through one entrance, followed by the old King DAVID, wearing his crown. ABIGAIL, TAMAR, BATHSHEBA, MICHAL and SOLOMON enter by another entrance. They process around the stage once, then DAVID speaks.

DAVID: Peace after war, there is a time for a reward,
     A time for trophies and a time for victories,
     An inspiration for my warlike urges.
     So many enemies conquered,
     So much food for the chronicles:
     The Assyrians, the Philistines, the Midianites –
     Victory in Gath, victory over Canaan,
     All the idolators, the desert's prey.
     Now to my glorious power, surpassing hyberbole,
     The Lion of Libya pays a shaggy tribute.
     The laurel turns to the vine, the wine is pressed,
     Brought to the banquet and drunk to the last dregs.
     Oh in my youth I clad my naked limbs
     In a vast bearskin, in curls and claws and hide,
     And tied its arms around my neck like jewels.
     Yes I was brave, and brave were my accomplishments,
     Which are engraved upon my body, all my old wounds.
     I lent you the gold of my youth and look –
     I am repaid now with these silver hairs.
     Every deed of war that is exchanged
     And all that passes is a kind of currency.
     For just one crown I plucked one day from the head
     Of the king of the Ammonites
     I am rewarded with four beautiful crowns
     Made from the eight arms of these wives of mine
     And what I wish, standing encircled like this,
     Is that I could grow three more necks, to wear four crowns
     And make Jerusalem into a theatre of love.
     Ruined is Rabbah, the court of the uncircumcised,
     The pride of the Ammonites, left to the ravages of time,
     And they trample the high mountains
     They cross the cerulean seas, weary and defeated.
     So this sadness of ours is transformed into laughter.
     Bellona, the war-goddess, is dead, and it is delightful
     To feel these four wreaths twining around me,
     Making me a new neck from your arms.
     Michal, my dear, for so many years
     You rewarded another man, someone unworthy of you,
     But love was fooled, envy avenged

And the historians got a tale they would love to tell.
You made me desire you –
Reward me now with devotion, with your embrace
Just as I rewarded you when I freed you from the Philistines
And your uncircumcised ways,
Giving a wise men a cause to write it all down,
Making an example for posterity.
Abigail! The wise one. The soother of angry breasts.
Once you were the undeserved, the unappreciated trophy
Of a barbarian peasant on Mount Carmel.
Let me rest in your arms in my old age.
Oh but I rest there now
And have done so for so long, I still feel young.
Bathsheba the beautiful – the bathing nymph,
Gazing upon your reflection in the water
You fell victim to my trickery.
It was a sin, and I have wept for it,
And you have made everything right again
After the wrong I did in killing Uriah the Hittite.
Yes, you have given us a son, a monarch for Israel,
Who can make peace in our time
And build a temple of the Ark of the Covenant:
Solomon my noble son, the famous architect.
The temple gives glory to God in the shape of a cloud.
Kindly and wise, the men of Hiram in Lebanon
Have given you cedarwood, so that the weather
Will never corrupt the sanctity of the law.
The people of Ophir sent gold, the men of Tarshish silver.
Tamar, my beautiful daughter, how are you?

TAMAR: Happy to have my mind restored to me.
    When you were away, I thought I was going to lose it.

ABIGAIL: My wish is granted. I rejoice to see you safe.

DAVID: Abigail, are you well?

ABIGAIL: Ready to serve you all my days.

DAVID: My beautiful Michal.

MICHAL: Glad to exchange sad sighs for laughter

43

Now you are here.

DAVID: Bathsheba!

BATHSHEBA: I offer you my soul. It springs to my eyes unbidden.

DAVID: This is the crown of the Ammonites. Feel it, it weighs
    More than a talent, or twenty thousand ducats.
    How beautiful it is. Now it is yours.
    You are the jewels in this crown of mine.
    My general Joab here, who has earned fame enough
    To crush all envy – he was the cause of my victory,
    He was the one who poisoned the wells in Rabbah
    And left his soldiers to complete the job
    And raze the thirsty city to the ground,
    Telling me afterwards, like a loyal subject,
    To take the credit for his victory.
    When Israel dedicates this conquest to me,
    You should give thanks instead to Joab.

JOAB: To kiss your feet will be reward enough
    For it means more to me to call myself your soldier
    And hang my trophies with your sacred weapons
    Before the Ark of the Covenant – trophies that sing
    The victory music of your harp.

DAVID: Talk to me Absalom, talk to me Adonijah,
    Expert in war and courteous in peace.

ABSALOM: How could the bravery of mere captains like us
    Compare with yours.

SOLOMON: Give us your arms.

ABIGAIL: These are auspicious times. The Hebrew flag
    Unites two men of mingled strength and beauty.

DAVID: Tell me about Amnon, how are things with him,
    My eldest son, the first fruit of my love?

ABIGAIL: He gives us great cause for concern, forever weeping
    And calling on death to come and cut his life short.
    He weeps, and he makes us mourn. He will not speak
    Of the reason for his sickness, and there is no one

44

Who can explain the pallor of his cheeks.

SOLOMON: None of the best doctors can diagnose
The cause of his depression. Nothing will distract him –
Music, hunting, none of the usual things.

BATHSHEBA: Amnon is crying out on the threshold of death,
And it will be a sad day for the kingdom.

ABIGAIL: You talk to him, and you may soothe his pain.
Here is his chamber.

*A curtain is drawn and AMNON is revealed sitting on a chair,
resting his cheek on his hand, dejected.*

DAVID: Now what is this, my beloved son and heir?
This is my victory day, and you're in mourning.
Come now, and have a look at the spoils.
Everyone's seen them except you.
I've been out there in the field.
I've conquered a kingdom for you,
Another kingdom!
Lift your head. Look up at me. Look!
Look at this crown, son, it matches your hair.
Take it. It's a gift. Look at me. Just once.
Do you want to kill me with your grief?

ABSALOM: Brother,
Your courtesy has never deserted you before
No matter what the cause for melancholy.
The King my lord and father is talking to you.

ADONIJAH: We know you are capable of love. Keep hold of it.
Speak to your father for your father's sake,
The king who weeps for you, who weeps before you.

SOLOMON: Don't put a curse upon this happy day.

ALL: Prince, come to your senses.

DAVID: Amnon!

AMNON: Oh for God's sake.

He looks up sadly.

45

They keep going on at me.

DAVID: ~~You are a copy of some sad original.~~
What's wrong?
I'll give you half of every Hebrew state
If it will make you well.
Take pleasure in what you have. Do not grieve like this.
Look at me. My only joy,
Your face is like a sun that has gone behind clouds.
Talk to me now and tell me what you want.

AMNON: I want you to go away and leave me alone.

DAVID: If that is what you want,
It's not for me to cause you further grief.
But remember, I shall be inconsolable.
You have spoilt the celebration
For all of Israel.
Don't I deserve something –
Even something insincere? A loving word.
Don't I deserve this? No. You think I don't.
I am an old man and now – now you are cruel to me.
What is it? What are you feeling? What do you want?

AMNON: I want you to go away and leave me alone.

ABSALOM: The wisest thing would be to leave him now.
He is impossible, intractable

DAVID: I've won a kingdom, but I've lost the Prince.
What is the point, my children, what is the point?

Exeunt. As TAMAR exits, AMNON calls to her and rises.

AMNON: Tamar, Tamar, my sister.

TAMAR: My lord?

AMNON: Listen, and I shall tell you the cause of this.
The King knows none of it.
Do you want to make me better?

TAMAR: If that's within my power, then Heaven knows
I would go visit wise old men and learn their remedies.
I'd seek out herbs and crystals, I'd climb mountains,

Anything to bring my prince back from the dead.

AMNON: Listen to this then. As long as you're not cruel
You'll need no crystals, drugs or herbs,
Mountains or wise old men.
My life is in your hands. It's trapped in your fingers.
Feel. Take my pulse. Put your fingers here.

She takes his hand.

Now you can feel the beating of my heart.

TAMAR: It feels irregular.

AMNON: That's because of my suffering.
Other people's veins carry blood. Mine carry fire.
Oh these hands touch the soul.

He takes her hands and kisses them.

And I pay for cruelty with kisses.
I wish I were made only of lips
So I might relish this moment more completely.

TAMAR: It is only as your sister I consent to these favours.

AMNON: Because this way you soothe my grief.

TAMAR: Enough of that. Tell me your sickness.

AMNON: I cannot do that. Fear puts a brake on the soul.
I want to tell you part of it. No. Leave.
I'd rather die in silence. Go away.

TAMAR: If you want me to go, I'll go.
Goodbye.

AMNON: What kind of cruelty is that? Wait.

TAMAR: I'm here.

AMNON: No, go.

TAMAR: That's enough of that.

AMNON: Come back.
I'll tell you of the beast that has me in its grasp.

TAMAR: If you won't trust your sister, what can I do?

AMNON: (*Aside.*) You are my sister and you are a woman.
   That is why I am going mad.

   To TAMAR.

   Couldn't you tell my sickness from my pulse?

TAMAR: I don't even know a doctor who could do that.
   Unless you tell me I shall never know.

AMNON: The pulse is the voice of the heart, but it talks in code.
   Sister, I'll tell you that this sickness of mine
   Lies between my name and yours.
   Isn't your name Tamar?

TAMAR: That is what they call me.

AMNON: Take away the T, and what will Tamar say?

TAMAR: *Amar.*

AMNON: *Amar* is my disease. My name is Amnon.
   Take out the Ns.

TAMAR: Your name would be *amo.*

AMNON: *Amo,* I love. *Amar,* to be in love.
   When you know this, what else do you need to know?
   I am in love, and that is my despair.
   That's my disease, to put your name by mine.

TAMAR: If we were linked in nature as in name,
   I'd perform miracles to make you well.

AMNON: Love is a correspondence between two persons.
   Is that not so?

TAMAR: Indeed, that's what they say.

AMNON: There not much difference between our names.
   Only two letters keep us apart. Why then
   Should I conceal my sickness, why not tell you?
   I have the means, I have the cure to hand.
   I'll tell you, Tamar.
   When we were up against the Ammonites,
   And I was there – second only to the King
   In combat, courage and in gallantry –

One evening, I glimpsed this woman on the ramparts,
A hymn to love and to love's mighty deeds,
And, though her eyes never met mine,
It was like being blinded by the sun.
I had become a foot-soldier in Love's army.
For the first time I understood some things
I'd wondered at before. My nights were sleepless
And I had doubts, suspicions, fantasies.
Jealousy spurred me on. I had to find out
Who it was who had done this thing to me.
I asked. I found out she was no less
Than the daughter of the barbarian King,
My enemy in blood and law. Blood and law!
Love sees these barriers as one: our law forbids
The mixing of Israelite and pagan blood.
So, seeing my love could never come to anything,
I decided I should get out of her sight
If it cost me my sanity. I returned to Jerusalem.
Day by day, my sickness grew worse
And nothing would distract me: hunting, gambling, talking –
Nothing would work. It came to such a pitch
That everything I asked for I detested.
I couldn't even remember what I'd once liked.
I waited for the King. There was one way
He could have given her to me as a wife.
Our law says that when a man loves as I did
And wants to take a bride he has won in combat
He must bring her home to his lands and to his house,
Remove her gentile clothing
And dress her up in the finest of our costume.
All that remains is to cut her nails and hair
And he can be her husband. I clung to this hope
And it was the one thing that kept me calm.
But now I know my father has levelled the city.
Bloodily, ruthlessly, he has razed it to the ground
And the woman I love is dead. Pity me, sister.
Pity me.

TAMAR: The greater your sickness, the more I feel your pain.
But how can I cure you, Amnon, how can I cure you?

AMNON: You could if you chose to, Tamar.

TAMAR: Tell me how.

AMNON: My passion is strange, but Eros is a child –
    He can be fooled, much as a child is fooled
    When he cries to his nurse for milk
    But lets some other woman give him suck.
    No harm is done. He's happy just being fed.
    It's like being tricked by an artificial flower –
    The colour, the form, the texture is the same.
    A man who loves fighting,
    Never so happy as when he's waging some war,
    He'll pick up a foil in peace and pretend to fight.
    I have known starving men get more satisfaction
    From cutting and carving meat than those who eat it.
    Love can be fooled, and my love too –
    You could deceive him, sister, if you wanted.
    You could pretend.
    If you could give him painted flowers,
    If you could offer the foil and let him fence,
    Out of harm's way, offer the war-drum in peace,
    Offer your breast while claiming it's another's,
    Love can be fooled. I could be fooled.
    And you could be the princess I have lost
    And call yourself by her name, and fall for me,
    Let me pursue you, write to you, weep for you,
    Pine for you, earn your respect, praise you to the skies
    And make demands on you. Since you're my sister,
    There'd be no scandal, no rumours of foul play.
    And you could help my passion run its course,
    Be like a fountain to ease the sick
    While never letting your waters touch my lips.

TAMAR: If that will bring you back your peace of mind,
    Go on and I shall try to play your lady.
    From now on, I shall cease to be your sister.
    Go on and woo me well. For the rest of this year
    I shall perform the role of your beloved.

AMNON: There is medicine in your words and in your tongue.

There is fortune in your hands.

Kisses her hands.

I am alive again and I can cure
My inner fire.

TAMAR: When you say that, are you talking to your lady
Or to Tamar?

AMNON: Till now to Tamar, but from now on
To the mirror of my love.

TAMAR: So I'm to stop being Tamar now.

AMNON: Yes, madam.

TAMAR: And I'm an Ammonite princess.

AMNON: And I have come to talk to you in your palace.
The King, your father, is distraught because
The King, my father, has laid siege to him.
I am ablaze with love.
I've told you, I shall be visiting you this night.
Now, here I come, furtively creeping through –

TAMAR: A secret doorway in the outer walls –

AMNON: And you come out to meet me, ready to show
How much you love me.

TAMAR: I like it. I'll begin acting.
But it'll be hard not to laugh.

Each withdraws a little from the other, and then AMNON re-enters, as though in darkness.

AMNON: Well then, I am here. This is the garden.
Even the trees weep at my grief. They weep
Amber condensed in drops of gold, they weep
Amber they gathered first from her bright glance.
The leaves are the eyes of the trees, and they are weeping.

TAMAR: Has my prince come? My dearest, is that you?

AMNON: Have I proved worthy? Will you honour me?

TAMAR: Are you alone?

AMNON: Love is unwise if it is not kept secret.
　　　　O my belovèd, give me what should be mine,
　　　　Those arms which I have paid for with my sighs,
　　　　And I will encircle you. We shall be like spheres,
　　　　Like shining spheres of love, of heavenly love.
　　　　I am a night sky, crowned with glorious signs –
　　　　Your eyes, your beautiful hair, your hands are stars –
　　　　A milky way that would make crystal envious.
　　　　But I am a slave to my imagination.
　　　　Hands, I will burn to ashes, I will burn –

He kisses her hands.

　　　　Unless you soothe my flames, unless you save me.

TAMAR: Slowly now, slowly.
　　　　I never said that you could go so far.

AMNON: Is that something you are saying to your brother
　　　　Or to your suitor who, driven wild with love,
　　　　Is humiliating himself here in your presence.

TAMAR: I say this to my brother and to my suitor
　　　　For if you really feel you are on fire,
　　　　That goes beyond the bounds of brotherly feeling.
　　　　And if a lady were to go so far
　　　　As to permit you to behave this way
　　　　On your first meeting – it would be presumptuous of you –
　　　　But that's enough for now. How do you feel?

AMNON: Better.

TAMAR: It's harmless playfulness, I suppose.

AMNON: It's love.

TAMAR: It's time you left.
　　　　There's something wrong with this.

AMNON: Aren't you my sister?

TAMAR: Yes, that is why you should show more respect.

AMNON: Dismiss me then as if I were a suitor.

TAMAR: Fine, if it makes you well.

AMNON: Farewell my sweetest treasure.

TAMAR: Farewell my noble lord.

AMNON: Do you love me very much?

TAMAR: I love you beyond measure.

AMNON: Do you accept my love?

TAMAR: Without a second thought.

AMNON: Do you love me as your lord?

TAMAR: I love you as I ought.

AMNON: Shall I come back tonight?

TAMAR: On the stroke of eleven.

AMNON: Will you forget my love?

TAMAR: No, by heaven.

AMNON: Are you sad to see me go?

TAMAR: I am overcome.

AMNON: And will you be unfaithful?

TAMAR: I tell you, no.
    I shall be like bronze.

AMNON: Will you sleep tonight?

TAMAR: Only to dream of you.

AMNON: What great fortune!

TAMAR: How sweet a dream!

AMNON: My dearest love.

TAMAR: My dearest lord.

AMNON: Delight of my eye.

TAMAR: Goodbye.

Exit AMNON. JOAB has been listening. He enters.

JOAB: *I love you beyond, measure. Shall I come back?*
    On the stroke of eleven, my dearest love...

What kind of talk is this? Is this brotherly love?
I heard what passed between you, and I don't think
This is the sort of language people use
Unless they're already lovers, Tamar.
I wanted to ask David for your hand
In payment for my valour in the war.
That was the only reason I did what I did,
Why I was the first to make the assault
Upon the walls at Zion –
That fatal moment for the Jebusites.
Then the King Prophet elevated me
To command the whole army, and that satisfied
The part of me that thought of fame and duty.
When I went out to the front line,
It was to prove myself to you. That's all.
Now I come back here and what is it I see?
Abominable blandishments of love
That offend against God, the King, your blood and the law.
My courtship of you is a thing of the past,
My love for you is ridiculed, my bravery
Goes unrewarded, and you, you are revealed
As thoroughly dishonoured and debauched.
At least, though, I have discovered this in time
To salvage what remains to me of honour.
I shall build a shrine to wise oblivion.
But first I shall go and tell the King what's happened,
What I have seen with my own eyes.
It seems that even as he's out there in the field
People at home are mocking his authority.
And as for you, you can take incestuous Amnon
As brother and husband. I shall learn to forget.

He makes to leave, but is held back by TAMAR.

TAMAR: Wait, valiant Joab. God grant you a long life.
But listen to the explanation of what you have seen,
And what will have seemed like love. When a man is mad
And starts to claim he's king and foams at the mouth,
A wise man plays along with it,
Calls him Your Majesty, and bows to him,

Greets him on bended knee. Amnon is mad,
So blind with love that he will probably die,
And that in turn, if it doesn't kill my father,
Will break the poor man's spirit in his old age.
My brother was in love with an Ammonite princess
Who died last week in the assault on Rabbah.
It's hopeless. She is imprinted on his soul.
He insists I am her double, and if I pity him
I must talk lover's talk to him when he's around.
He is my brother. I know very well
The power of the blind passion that so destroys him,
And so, to help alleviate his madness,
I've been going along with him, humouring him,
And that was what you saw. But let me say this:
If what I've been doing is going to injure you
Or put a question-mark against my reputation,
I'd much prefer that Amnon my brother died
Than have you fret about this one more day.
He's hurt. He has known love. But I love too
And my beloved is the most gallant captain
Jerusalem ever saw. Go to my father,
Go to my father now and ask for my hand.
He's given his daughters to much lesser men.
Whatever you do, don't let this game, this stratagem
Created to deceive a very sick man,
Lead you to doubt my constancy or my love.
Are you calmer now?

JOAB: Calm, yes, and much ashamed
To have been so stupid as to have ever thought
Such things of you. I know how wise you are.
I value your honesty and delight in your good name.
An end to jealousy, an end to anger –
Will Tamar forgive her Joab? From this day
I swear I will not believe or trust what I see
As long as I intend to be your husband.

TAMAR: And that will be reward enough for my love.

JOAB: Until that bond is sealed, let me kiss your hand.

AMNON enters as JOAB kisses her hand before leaving.

AMNON: The cup the Prince drinks from – it is his alone.
    His horse is his alone, his clothing, his royal seat,
    All his alone. And the hand the Prince has kissed
    Is his alone – for a subject to dare to kiss it,
    That's treason. You have injured me as a brother
    And as a lover you enrage me, sister.
    Do you want to drive me mad, drive me to revenge?
    Oh I shall kill him, I shall kill your Joab
    And even if you deny your fickleness
    The hand he kissed shall give your lips the lie.

TAMAR: Amnon, enough of this – it's gone too far,
    This playing your sister now, and now your loved one
    When one thing is true and one is an illusion.
    Give up these chimaeras and forget your passion.
    I am destroying my reputation for your health.
    This person you keep seeing in me, this princess,
    She's dead. And me, I'm dead too – dead to your love.
    Stop talking to me in this deceitful code.
    Joab and I are in love. Our love is honest.
    But the woman you loved and I are far too close
    And I can't see how you will satisfy yourself
    Without giving one or other of us offence.

Exit TAMAR.

AMNON: How can you leave me like this, you murderer,
    Looking so calm and indifferent,
    As if you had just untied a bandage
    And left my life to seep away.
    Cruel Tamar, inconstant Tamar,
    I shall have my revenge.

Enter JONADAB.

JONADAB: What is it, my Lord?

AMNON: I am sick with jealousy.

JONADAB: Jealous of whom? May I know?

AMNON: Since I am dying, yes.
>   I cannot hold my tongue, nor do I wish to.
>   I am consumed with love for Tamar.

JONADAB: What?

AMNON: I don't want your advice. You might as well kill me.

JONADAB: That is a lunatic love.
>   And yet you know I am your faithful servant
>   And, being so, I hate to hear you complain.
>   I'll do my best for you. Your life can be saved
>   But only at the cost of Tamar's honour.
>   Pretend you are ill and confined to bed.

AMNON: There's no pretence in this torture.

JONADAB: Hide your desires.
>   You know how David loves you. Call for the King.
>   Ask him to send your sister here to feed you
>   And when she is here, alone, and in your power –
>   Well, I need say no more. You are no fool.
>   You'll know how to seize the opportunity, when it comes.

AMNON: That would be a cure,
>   That would be a new life for me, or perdition.
>   Go get my father. What are you waiting for?

JONADAB: Love's blind, and cannot tell one colour from another.
>   It knows no frontier between a sister and a brother.

Exit JONADAB.

AMNON: What if the blood is hot, and no flame near?
>   What will the blood do, if it burns like mine?
>   What if my blood burns for love of my own flesh and blood?
>   What is the law that says: like shall not love like?
>   The sons of Adam, the daughters of Eve –
>   Didn't they love as I love? Were they not siblings?
>   It is the law that is unnatural.
>   Like loves like – that is the natural law.

Enter DAVID, JONADAB and ELIAZER.

DAVID: As soon as I heard that you had sent for me,

I felt alive again. I was consoled.
Speak freely. Ask me whatever you want.

AMNON: Oh father, I am so weak I shall soon die
Unless your grace prevents it. There is nothing,
Nothing I can bear to eat, to tempt my appetite,
Nothing that will restore my health to me.
Still, the sick are irrational. I know that.
And I think if Tamar were simply to come here,
If she so much as glanced at a plate of stew
Or handed me some nourishing thing to drink,
She might give me reason to live
Although, as you see, it may be already too late.
Would you, sir?
Would you grant me this favour?

DAVID: You ask so little of my love.
If this will cure your sadness, Tamar will come.
She will look after you.

AMNON: I kiss your feet.

DAVID: All is well.

AMNON: She cooks to my taste. Tamar's the only one,
The only one who understands my needs.

DAVID: I'll not have you wait another moment.
I'll call the Princess myself.

Exit DAVID.

AMNON: Talk to me, Eliazer, sing to me
If singing can calm love.

ELIAZER: (*Sings.*) *She walks down to the river.*
She passes through the reeds.
The dawn among the roses
Weeps at what it sees.

Her footprints are of amber.
The flowers are full of dew.
They reach for her as she passes
As she comes walking through –

> *As she walks down to the river*
> *While the city sleeps*
> *As the roses reach to catch her*
> *And the dawn, the dawn weeps.*

Enter TAMAR, a towel over her shoulder, carrying a silver tray holding two silver dishes.

TAMAR: The King my Lord has sent me to you
    To bring you something to eat with my own hand
    Since I'm the one who knows your tastes.
    But I'm afraid this food will seem unseasoned.
    They say that salt is another name for good will.
    I've little enough of that just now.

AMNON: Jonadab, leave the room.
    And close the door behind you, Eliazer.
    This food my soul has been longing for –
    I shall taste it alone.

TAMAR: Think first what you are doing.

AMNON: You are so selfish. This is no time for thinking.
    It is time for you to become the food,
    Food for the soul you have let starve so long.

TAMAR: Dear brother, though you can scarcely be dear to me,
    If you should be so cruel, you are a Prince of Israel
    And all our people live under your protection.
    My honour is as clear as a mirror.
    I look in it and recognise my worth.
    If you try to break it, I will not allow you.
    You will only earn yourself a name
    As an inept and stupid lover.
    Remember I am of your blood.

AMNON: And that is why I love you.

TAMAR: Calm yourself.

AMNON: I will not be calmed.

TAMAR: What do you want?

AMNON: I want Tamar.

TAMAR: Let go.

AMNON: Remember I am Amnon.

TAMAR: What if I call the King?

AMNON: I shall call to Eros.

TAMAR: Can you do this to your sister?

AMNON: I want to make love to you.

TAMAR: You are betraying me.

AMNON: There's no injustice in love.

TAMAR: The law.

AMNON: Love knows no law.

TAMAR: Think of the King.

AMNON: Love is my king.

TAMAR: Think of your honour.

AMNON: My honour is whatever I want it to be.

Exeunt

ACT THREE

Enter AMNON, throwing TAMAR out of his room.

AMNON: Get out, get out of here you golden cup of poison,
    Beautiful-seeming sepulchre, fine-featured harpy.
    Revolting animal, venom in your eyes,
    Do not look, do not spit on me. You are trying to kill me.
    Monster get out, before you put the evil eye on me
    And ruin what is left of my youth.
    Did I love you? Did I? Did I favour you once,
    You fruit of Sodom, you horrible Sodom-apple?
    Heart of coal in a skin of silk, get out!
    Oh you are the terror of my life, you are my punishment.
    My first love, were you? I hate you the more for that.
    Throw her out!

TAMAR: What you are doing now, the offence, the injury,
    Is worse than what you did in the climax of your love.
    You are a tyrant in a prince's body. You are trying
    To double my dishonour before I have a chance for revenge.
    When a woman has been used like this, she's nothing but trash.
    I'm trash to you. Have me thrown out in the street
    Now you've had your way with me, with my honour,
    Throw me to the dogs; give the whole pack of strays a turn
    To lick the dish you've eaten from, then cast away.
    This dress of mine you've just ripped apart, give it to your
        servant.
    Divide the spoils of my honour – share them out among your
        servants
    Anything to give me the greater cause for rage.

AMNON: I would that I'd been born without ears, born without
        eyes
    So I might never see or hear from you again.
    Go away, woman.

TAMAR: Thank you.
    And where do you think I'm going to go without my honour?

A woman without her honour is like a merchant without his
    goods.
Even if you have forgotten yourself,
You can pay more attention to your sister.
Don't just pile crime upon crime.
Whoever does that will perish on a chain of sin.
You have gambled with my honour, you have played me false
You have won my precious jewels from me, and I want them
    back.
But it's too late to ask for them back.
Take my life. Why not? I've lost everything else
Everything that was precious to me – except one thing.
Don't get up from the gaming table quite so quickly.
My losses are great, and losers are always bad company,
But the noble man will never leave the game
Until there is nothing left to lose.
I still have my life left, but it is a life without honour
And I intend to lose it on the next throw.
Finish the game, traitor, and kill me on the cheap.

AMNON: The flames of hell are freezing over
    And you torment me still.
    Serpent, monster, get out of here.

TAMAR: The loser takes insults willingly –
    It's the price of staying in the game.
    Play on, tyrant, until I have done with losing.
    Raise your hand, villain, and take my life –
    That way you will have won the hand.

AMNON: Was there ever such torture? Is there no one out there?
    Is this the cost of a moment of madness?

Enter ELIAZER and JONADAB.

ELIAZER: You called?

AMNON: Throw out this viper, this pestilence.

ELIAZER: Viper? Pestilence? What's wrong with her?

AMNON: Take her away from me and shut the door behind her.

JONADAB: Tamar is like a piece of paper now. He has read her

And now he wants to tear her up.

AMNON: Throw her into the street.

TAMAR: Do that exactly, for though the crime was here
It's right I should go crying through the streets
Telling how you dishonoured me.

AMNON: I won't listen to any more of this.

Exit.

JONADAB: This is a strange thing, Eliazer,
That such a hatred should follow so much love.

TAMAR: Peasant, you will soon see how Tamar is avenged.

Exeunt.

Enter ABSALOM and ADONIJAH.

ABSALOM: Ambitious man, if you were not my brother,
And if we were not here in my father's palace,
I'd put a stop to all your aspirations,
Your shamelessness and your life too.

ADONIJAH: And if my father's blood did not flow in your veins,
Though you are far from worthy of that purple,
I'd see you bleed till you bled dry
And wear that royal purple on my feet.

ABSALOM: Madman and slave, you are seeking to be king.
When Amnon dies of the sickness that's consuming him,
Your plan is to ascend the sovereign throne,
The symbol of the valour of the Twelve Tribes.
I am your elder brother – didn't you know that?
What man would dare compete with Absalom?
Fortune herself has laid riches at my feet,
Valour and beauty too.

ADONIJAH: Valour and beauty!
If it were true that the Kingdom of Israel
Always passed to the handsomest in line, the prettiest prince,
Then it is true – though I myself am no monster –
The nation would bow its neck beneath your yoke.

Each of our tribes would fall under the enchantment,
Entangled in the golden Ophir of your hair.
There would be an end to war, the age of frivolity would begin
With ribbons for taxes and cosmetics for tributes,
Your council would consist entirely of women,
Your crown – a crown of hair, your famous father's throne
A daybed, a divan.
Instead of armour, you would buckle on brocade,
You shield would be a mirror and your sword a fan.
All eyes are upon you, for Nature made you the elder son
And heaven has bestowed a fortune on your head.
Every year, when the weight of it is too much to bear,
You make a harvest of your crowning glory
And sell your hair to the ladies,
Hawking your wares around the tents.
Two hundred shekels a lock!
Go on; be lord and master of your beauty.
But leave Israel to me. You might do yourself a damage,
Your soft, delicate –

ABSALOM: Peasant, hold your insolent tongue.
Yes, you are envious, but a wise man said
That beauty holds the key to good governance
Since it reveals the noble soul within.
A beautiful guest lives in a beautiful house.
Now when my father sets off on his campaigns
I don't stay behind at court, wasting my life.
When it comes to the battlefield I'm not found wanting:
My sword is bright with the blood of the uncircumcised.
Priests are idle in war, but I have shown
Courage and beauty keep good company.
But why should I justify such an evident truth.
If my beauty makes me a coward, your sword can prove it.

ADONIJAH: You only wear that thing for decoration.
Don't touch it. That way you'll stay safe.
If you pull it out you might faint.

ABSALOM: If the King weren't coming…

ADONIJAH: If the King weren't coming…

64

Enter King DAVID and SOLOMON.

DAVID: Your mother has petitioned me, Solomon,
    On your behalf. Grow now, become a man.
    If you are favoured as your name foretells,
    You will ascend the royal throne, and your fame
    Will astonish men across the ages. I hope so.

SOLOMON: My lord, such praise will only fall to me
    If I resemble you.

DAVID: Princes.

ABSALOM: My lord?

DAVID: What are you discussing?

ADONIJAH: How peace is a time for frivolous novelties,
    How the young squander everything on clothes,
    And truth brings disillusionment to the old.

ABSALOM: We were planning to go off hunting on our own,
    So that we don't fall victim to idleness.
    We were talking of that. And a party afterwards.

DAVID: Great God, what is all that shouting?

Enter TAMAR, her hair loose and dressed in mourning.

TAMAR: O King of Israel, of the line of the lion of Judah,
    The lion that Jacob gave to avenge a nation's wrongs,
    Will tears move you? Will sighs, will a faltering voice,
    Will my insults move you, the fact I am your daughter.
    Will they move you to compassion, will they move you to
        punish
    The man who has offended against your blood?
    I am your daughter and I pour out my soul through my eyes,
    I sigh to heaven, I am in mourning –
    I am in mourning for the honour I have lost.
    I have put ashes on my head, ashes,
    For a wild love is a fire and a fire leaves ashes on the wind,
    But ashes are only ashes, they cannot cleanse the stain.
    Blood, yes, blood is good for a soap.
    Blood will wash my honour clean.

Prince Amnon's disease – it was a plague of honour,
And the contagion has been passed on to me.
You commanded me yourself to cook him a dish,
Something to revive his faltering appetite,
But it would have been better to prepare him a poison.
I gave him a nourishing meal, but nourishing food
Is nothing if the sickness corrupts the appetite itself.
His hunger lay in his soul, and to my misfortune
He made me a feast of wrong. He had no shame.
The very chance was like a spice to him. He paid no heed
To my protests, to my cries. I reminded him
I am the daughter of the King. I am his sister.
But he cared nothing for his duty, his law, his God.
He sent his companions away. Then he broke the lock
Of the temple of my reputation
And he defiled the sanctuary of my honour.
He violated me. And at once he grew to hate me.
And that does not surprise me, since, in the end,
Possession is the enemy of desire.
He forced himself on me and then he threw me from his house,
And he spat insults after me,
Paying for his pleasure with words of hatred.
It was all the payment I could have expected from such a man.
I walked out into the street. I was dishonoured
And the people of Jerusalem – they heard my cries.
The very stones of the roads consoled each other.
The sun hid its rays in the clouds rather than see
Such an atrocity. Everyone is calling to you for justice.
Justice! My lord. No one ever conquered you.
You will say that Amnon is of your blood.
His vice has corrupted your blood. Bleed yourself dry of him
If you want your good name to survive.
You have other sons who could inherit the crown,
Sons who are like you in virtue and in strength.
Do not keep a successor to the throne
Who despises your reputation
And who shows it by dishonouring his sister,
For such a man will only treat his subjects
With even greater disrespect.

Think of the generous blood of Abraham. He had one son
But he was brave enough to raise the knife over him.
He had one son, and you have many.
Isaac was innocent. Amnon is not.
That was the way that Abraham served his God
And in this way you too will serve your God.
O my unconquered King, conquer yourself,
Put justice before love and earn a greater glory
Than when you killed the lion.
Brothers, my brothers, plead with me for justice.
Beautiful Absalom, we were conceived by one father
And one mother bore us. The others are my half-brothers
And only half disgraced in my dishonour.
We share a father and a mother. Demand justice for me
Or from now on live without honour, injured forever.
Father, brothers, people of Israel,
I cry to the streets, the doorways, to the sky, to the sun,
I cry to the beasts of the field, to the fish, to the trees,
To the fields, to the elements, to God on high.
Amnon has violated his sister. He has broken the law.
All of you, all of you, bring him to justice.

DAVID: Princess, get up from the ground.
Call Prince Amnon to me.
O heaven, is this what it is to have children?
Grief makes me dumb. Let my eyes speak for me
And feel my sorrow, and let them be tongues to me.
Let my tears be words to explain what is in my heart.
The Law calls me King, but Love names me the father.
One urges, one obliges me – which one will win?

ABSALOM: Sister, I wish to God you had never been my sister.
Be reasonable. There's no way you can be avenged.
Amnon, who is your brother and of your blood,
Has brought this whole offence upon himself.
This insult to me, this dishonour of yours
Must now be kept within these four walls.
I have a home in Ephraim, farmland in Baal-hazor.
They were meant for pleasure once,
Now they will house your grief.

You will live with me there. A fallen woman
Cannot stay at court with her reputation gone.
Let's go to Ephraim and see if time is a wise doctor
And can relieve your suffering, make you forget.

TAMAR: You are right. Better to live among animals
If you have lost your honour among men.
At least in such a company I shall know
I cannot lose my honour yet again.

Exit TAMAR.

ABSALOM: Amnon, you incestuous tyrant,
Absalom will soon demand satisfaction in full.
I'll have your kingdom and I'll have your life.

Exit ABSALOM.

ADONIJAH: There are no words, there is no reasoning
No comfort, no advice in such a sad case.
I'm going. I don't know what to think.

Exit ADONIJAH.

SOLOMON: The Princess is my sister, the Prince my brother.
I grieve for the wrong done to the one. I fear for the other.
What's happened is horrible, but the King is a prudent man.
Best to let time and wonder do what work they can.

Exit SOLOMON. Enter AMNON fearful. DAVID is weeping.

AMNON: The King my lord has sent for me. Shall I go?
How will I dare to look upon his face
Without fear and shame. I tremble at the snow
Of all that silver hair. It reminds me that sin
Is the ashes of the fire love set ablaze.
How spirited the sinner can be,
Before succumbing to vice.
What a coward he turns into
After the deed is done.

DAVID: Prince?

AMNON: I throw myself at your feet.

He kneels at a great distance from DAVID.

DAVID: (*Aside.*)

    Shouldn't justice have more influence here than love?

    I am his father, but I am the King.

    He is my son, but he was the guilty party.

    His eyes plead. The Princess demands revenge.

    I should arrest him as a warning to others

    Against this kind of conduct. But the boy is pale –

    He's only just recovering from his sickness

    And I can feel he's afraid. What's this?

    What has become of my old strength of purpose?

    And what will Israel say of such foolish weakness?

    Let justice live. Let the prince die.

    Amnon!

AMNON: My loving father.

DAVID: Loving father

    He calls me, and the words cut me to the quick.

    He pleads to my loving heart. But he must die.

He turns to him, enraged, but he no sooner sees him than he is softened.

    How are you, son?

AMNON: Better today, my father, through your mercy.

DAVID: Each time I look at him, my rage becomes

    Like wax in the blazing sunlight of his face.

    And I remember once the highest judge

    Pardoned me for adultery and murder –

    Pardoned me, even though I was the King,

    Because I had repented from the heart.

    Pity overcame the rigour of his mind,

    And I am made in His own image.

    The left hand deals punishment, the right forgiveness.

    Maybe left-handedness is a defect.

To AMNON.

    Prince, be very careful. Be mindful of your position.

    Ah, joy of my heart!

Exit DAVID. AMNON rises.

AMNON: Oh Love, you are the power, the only God,
     For only Love has ever conquered David,
     The King, the conqueror. He told me to be careful –
     Feeble advice, but the unspoken reprimand
     Should be reproof enough for a prudent man.
     He was afraid to give me pain. I see
     And understand how to repay his love
     By never more offending against his will.

Exit AMNON. Enter ABSALOM.

ABSALOM: He didn't speak a single word to him in anger?
     Never so much as an angry look?
     Tamar's his daughter – though Amnon is his son.
     It doesn't matter. I am now determined
     To have the vengeance that eludes my father
     Since he is blinded by the passion of love.
     Only when Amnon dies will basic justice
     Be satisfied and my ambition with it.
     It is not right for a man to rule a kingdom
     If he cannot control his appetites.
     His crime and my advancement are reason enough
     For me to act. I am David's second son
     But Amnon's crime makes me the first-born.
     I'll have a word with my father. I shall wake him
     From the enchantment love has trapped him in.
     He's coming. But what is this?

He draws aside a curtain, revealing a desk on which there is a platter, and on that a golden crown.

     The crown that should encircle the royal brow
     Of my wise father, left here on a platter?
     This is the dish I have been longing for
     So much, so long. It is an invitation.
     Power tastes good, so the ambitious claim,
     And here's a tasty morsel not to be missed.
     Crown of my hopes, Amnon will not enjoy you
     For you are made of gold. He should wear
     A baser metal – he dishonoured Tamar.
     I would request you to do me such an honour

As to encircle my head, but I'm afraid
You would refuse. Though you would crown the picture,
You would be fearful that I might outshine you
With my golden hair.

He places the crown on his head.

You suit me well. You might say
I was born to wear you. That's no disrespect.
For I am born of royal blood and you
Were born for me to wear. Will I prove worthy?
Yes. Will I manage to keep you? Yes again.
Who in Jerusalem will try to stop me? Amnon?
I'll kill him. Would my father seek revenge?
I'll kill my father!

DAVID: Who would you kill?

DAVID draws his sword and advances on ABSALOM. He finds him wearing his crown.

ABSALOM: Heaven help me.
Kill any man who would not serve Your Highness.

ABSALOM kneels.

DAVID: Your head is crowned. Why are you at my feet?

ABSALOM: My brother is ill. I thought I might inherit.

DAVID: You are too eager. You will not succeed me.
That crown is worth a talent, I would reckon.
You are not worthy of it… and you would kill me?

ABSALOM: Me?

DAVID: Were you not saying that?

ABSALOM: If you had heard me clearly,
You would be praising my loyalty. What I said
Was that if I should ever come to the throne,
And you were alive, still, in Jerusalem,
I'd bring to trial anyone accused of treachery,
Anyone, I was saying, who would *kill my father.*

DAVID: I see. But is there anyone you know

Who fits that description?

ABSALOM: No one. Although
A man who could rape his sister could kill his father.

DAVID: Tamar is your full sister. That is why
You have taken against Amnon. But listen to me:
No enemy of Amnon's is a friend of mine.

ABSALOM: You are unfair to be angry like this with me.
Am I the only one who finds you cruel?

DAVID: What does it matter, if you are cruel to Amnon?

ABSALOM: No one in Israel loves Amnon more than I do.
Indeed I was about to invite your Highness with him,
And all the other princes of the blood
To the shearing festival at Baal-hazor,
Hoping that he would honour me with his presence.
So far from any foolish thought of revenge,
I have already prepared a banquet there
Worthy of such a guest. Sir, with your presence,
Honour our fleece and let yourself be distracted
From the grief caused by this wretched turn of events.
Amnon will soon understand: all that I want
Is the harvest of his love.

DAVID: If you forget,
If you forgive the Prince for what he has done,
You'll see his life return, you'll be a phoenix,
You'll be an Abel, not a cowardly Cain.

ABSALOM: If I should ever seek revenge on him,
Let the whole world turn on me. If I betray you,
Let me be hung by my hair and let me die
Caught between earth and sky.

DAVID: Do as you say
And I'll forgive you all your youthful follies
And I shall crown you with a better crown
Than this one. I shall crown you with my arms.

ABSALOM: Sir, let me kiss your feet. Will you but add
To all the mercies you have heaped upon me

By saying that you're happy with my plan,
That you agree to attend and honour my feast,
Since respite from the war gives you the leisure
And you will find good cheer there, I assure you.

DAVID: We would be only one expense too many.
No, son, enjoy the fruits of your farm yourself.
Old age demands I wear out these last grey hairs
Attending to the kingdom.

ABSALOM: If my pleas
Are not enough to win that honour from you,
Give leave at least and lend your voice to mine
In asking that Solomon, Amnon and Adonijah
Go to my farm to taste the extent of my love.

DAVID: Amnon? Not him, my son.

ABSALOM: He is despondent.
The fields, the river, the shearing of the sheep
Will be a distraction from his grief.

DAVID: I am afraid
Anything untoward might give me new cause for tears.

ABSALOM: I'm sorry you should have so little faith in my love.

DAVID: I go by my own experience in this.
The enemy is always at his most dangerous
When an attack comes in disguise of peace.

ABSALOM: Then I shall have to earn your trust, I see,
By showering him with favours and with gifts.
I'll seek to do so.

DAVID: There's no harm in caution.

ABSALOM: May I be hanged on the common gallows tree
The day I cause Prince Amnon any harm.
I shall not rise from before you, father,
Until you allow Amnon to come to me.

DAVID: He is the greatest treasure of my soul.
And yet, to demonstrate how much I trust you,
I will allow it.

ABSALOM: Now I am certain of your love.

DAVID: (*Aside.*) What is this doubt, this chill of fear?

ABSALOM: I shall go at once and let him know.

DAVID: Any thought of harm you had, put it behind you.

ABSALOM: Don't be afraid.

DAVID: Oh Absalom, my son,
    This is the way you test how much I love you.

ABSALOM: Goodbye.

DAVID: Remember that you take half my heart with you.

Exeunt DAVID and ABSALOM. Enter TIRSO, BRAULIO, ALISO, RISELO, ARDELIO, SHEPHERDS, and TAMAR dressed as a shepherdess, her face covered by a veil. They sing.

SHEPHERDS: *The sheep and rams are bleating.*
        They're waiting to be fleeced.
        So listen to our greeting.
        And come and join the feast.
        For we are simple herdsmen.
        We will not keep you long.
        But we have come to sing you
        A simple fleecing song.

        The simple man goes courting.
        He's not got much to show.
        She looks at him cavorting.
        She doesn't want to know.
        She ought to tell him simply
        To try his luck elsewhere.
        He's ugly and he's pimply.
        She'll fleece him then and there.

        The message is so simple.
        The message is the same.
        If you forget the message
        You'll have yourself to blame.

        The simple man is toothless –
        He cannot read or write.

The scribe is rich and ruthless –
He can fleece him overnight.
The prisoner in the dungeons
Hauled up before the mayor
Will lose his shirt and long-johns.
They'll fleece him then and there.

The message is so simple.
The message is the same.
If you forget the message
You'll have yourself to blame.

To put the matter simply
So there is no mistake.
The nun is wise and wimply.
The monk is on the make.
The priest who hears confession,
The bishop on his chair
Do not think it transgression
To fleece you then and there.

The message is so simple.
The message is the same.
If you forget the message
You'll have yourself to blame.

The shepherd in the May time
Is not unlike his sheep.
He wants it in the daytime.
He wants it in his sleep.
He wants a word with Cupid
About a love affair
But the god of love's not stupid –
He'll fleece him then and there.

The message is so simple.
The message is the same.
If you forget the message
You'll have yourself
And nobody else –
You'll have yourself to blame.

TIRSO: The cows that drink from Jordan's crystal streams
　　　　And graze on the salt thyme will be blessed today
　　　　At the sight of your beauty, as you come walking by.
　　　　However much the sun has dried them out,
　　　　The meadows will put forth fresh grass again.
　　　　Beautiful Tamar, what is it makes you disconsolate
　　　　When you can make the hills themselves happy?
　　　　They say the court is wherever is the King.
　　　　Since you're the queen of beauty, this must be
　　　　Your court. There's no way round it.
　　　　Little princess, relax, enjoy yourself.
　　　　Dare to admire your beauty in the water.
　　　　It's offering itself to you as a mirror..

TAMAR: I am afraid to look at my reflection.

BRAULIO: If that's because you're afraid of falling in love
　　　　With your own face, you're right. I swear
　　　　You've put everyone here in a muck sweat
　　　　From their souls to their vital organs.
　　　　It was an ill day the devil brought you here.
　　　　But look and see how well your portrait is drawn
　　　　On the surface of the river. It would make a painting,
　　　　With golden and blue flowers to frame and adorn it.

TAMAR: You call me beautiful but I am stained.
　　　　And if I saw that pollution I would cry.

ALISO: Stained, are you? There are mirrors here
　　　　That hide the stains they see. We teach them kindness.
　　　　It is at court mirrors show only flaws,
　　　　That hit you in the face when you look in the glass.
　　　　But there are mirrors of water here,
　　　　And though they see the stains they wash them clean.

TAMAR: If water could remove this stain, my tears
　　　　Would be enough. I've shed enough of them.
　　　　But only the blood of a disloyal man
　　　　Can wash me clean.

RISELIO: I've never heard of that.
　　　　They go for virgin honey here. It's like

76

Daubing your face with your virginity.
Spots, is it?

TAMAR: In a way. They are spots on my honour.

ARDELIO: Cover them with mercury.

TAMAR: There's no mercury left.
Shepherd, my life is already drenched with poison.

TIRSO: Is it a birthmark you're hiding with that veil?

TAMAR: Like something one is born with, it will not change.
But what dishonours me is not a birthmark.

TIRSO: Whatever it is, let's sing.
Singing is good for lifting gloom.
Anything else is foolish.

They sing.

SHEPHERDS: *It's a song for a sad Infanta.*
It's a song that the shepherds sing.
It's a song for a woman who sorrows.
Saying: Time heals everything.

For the bitterest words of the lover
There's a cure in a moment apart.
In the pain of a broken illusion
A change is good for the heart.

Is it jealousy so torments you?
Make him jealous and leave him be.
But remember when age is upon you
To lay down your arms and be free.

There are books to be read in the study
To study your way out of grief.
Is revenge such a cure for your honour?
Forgiving can bring relief.

It's a song for a sad Infanta.
It's a song that the shepherds sing.
It's a song for the woman who sorrows.
Saying: Time heals everything.

> *Saying: Time is where we live.*
> *Saying: Time is where we forgive.*
> *Saying:Time heals everything.*

Enter LAURETA with a basket of flowers.

LAURETA: This basket is full of herbs, jasmine and roses,
   The freshest and the loveliest flowers – thyme,
   Carnations, purple plantain, Sweet William,
   The violet Cupid treads on for its scent,
   Columbine, wallflower, lilies and broom.
   Take them. I've sacked the countryside for its spoils.
   Take them and press them to your lips, your hair,
   Your breasts, your brow, eyelashes and eyes.

TAMAR: The loveliest flower of April
   Would soon begin to pall.
   Laureta, I have lost the flower
   That mattered most of all.

LAURETA hands TAMAR some violets, and she places them at her breast.

TIRSO: Laureta,
   You'll manage to find some dreams or crazy stories
   To comfort Tamar. Everyone says you're a witch
   And you have dealings with the devil.

ARDELIO: The Princes arrived today, to pay a visit
   And give us a blessing.

TIRSO: What are you waiting for?

ARDELIO: While they are settling in,
   Let's go to the wood and gather flowers and greenery
   To decorate the house.

TIRSO: You are right, Ardelio.
   But what flowers could match the beauty of Absalom?

Exeunt the SHEPHERDS.

TAMAR: We should go now, Laureta.

LAURETA: Why? You are well enough disguised.

TAMAR: But badly hurt.

LAURETA: You will forget that wrong if you are wise.

TAMAR: That's good advice. But it was a wise man who said:
'The cure was to forget, but she forgot the cure.'

Enter AMNON, ABSALOM, ADONIJAH and SOLOMON.

AMNON: This landscape is beautiful.

ABSALOM: Yes, it is May
The courting month, there are flowers everywhere.

ADONIJAH: More like the labouring month. My clothes are ripped.

AMNON: Hey, there are some country girls. They don't look bad.

ABSALOM: They are from my estate. The women of the court
Envy their artless beauty.

AMNON: Lucky the girl who owes her beauty to nature
And not to make-up and fine dresses.

ABSALOM: *That* woman has the gift. She can tell the future.
These country people take her for a witch.

SOLOMON: Is that significant?

AMNON: It's foolish to pay attention to these people.
She might tell one true thing in twenty lies.
But who is her companion – the one with the veil?

ABSALOM: She is a beautiful shepherdess, in mourning
For her lost honour, waiting for revenge.

AMNON: She's very striking. May we not see her face?

ABSALOM: She has decided she will wear the veil
Until her honour is restored.

AMNON: What wonderful determination.

To LAURETA.

Well I shall turn to you. Come here, my girl.

LAURETA: Your Highness? You will court first, then run away.

AMNON: Indeed you look as if you had second sight.

You have all these flowers, why don't you share them out,
If you would be so kind?

LAURETA: These fields are Amaltheia's theatre.
I shall give each of you on flower.

AMNON: Can't your friend speak? Take off your veil.

LAURETA: She has taken a vow of silence.

AMNON: Silence? What for?

LAURETA: Her honour.

AMNON: Is there honour among peasants?

LAURETA: It is all the stronger. Here there are no princes,
Nor easy ladies of the court. But enough of that.
Here are your flowers.

AMNON: Which is mine?

LAURETA: (*Speaking to each aside.*) This lily.

She gives him a lily with a pointed reed.

AMNON: That must be as a mark of my honesty.

LAURETA: I know you like the scent. But do not tear it.
It has a leaf here, sharp, like a sword.
The pollen on these golden tips, though it please the eye,
Will stain you if you handle it. Don't touch it.
The treasure of this flower is its intactness.
And, Amnon, if you pull apart this flower
That grows among the razor-sharp reeds of honour,
And if you harm it, you had better watch out.

AMNON: I value your advice. (This woman's a demon.)

SOLOMON: What she say?

AMNON: Pay no attention. She's mad.

ADONIJAH: Which flower's for me?

LAURETA: A strange one. Larkspur. Here.

She hands him a blue larkspur.

80

ADONIJAH: I like it well for the name.

LAURETA: Sometimes a spur
Can injure the man who wears it.

ADONIJAH: I'm a skilled rider.

LAURETA: You're a skilled rider, then I will hold my peace.
But watch out if you chance to take a fancy
To a married woman. Do not, in striving high,
Allow yourself to fall.

ADONIJAH: I don't understand.

ABSALOM: I shall go last. Solomon. Take your turn.

SOLOMON: Both of them came away looking perplexed.

To LAURETA.
If there is any way I can persuade you,
Tell me more plainly what you mean.

LAURETA: We call this flower king's crown. Enjoy its properties.
It's beautiful, fragrant and it's valuable.
Learn from it then. You too will be a king –
The greatest of them all. But I'm afraid
The flowers of love may prove your eventual downfall
If you should still feel young when you are old.

AMNON: A handsome flower.

SOLOMON: Handsome, but it has thorns.

ABSALOM: Now, which is to be mine.

LAURETA: For you, this narcissus.

She gives him a narcissus.

ABSALOM: Narcissus fell in love with his reflection.

LAURETA: Pay heed then to his story, Absalom,
And do not love yourself so much
Or you will cause all Israel to despise you
With your self-love, your boasting and your arrogance.
Your nation is made helpless at the sight of you,
Absalom and you have the same effect

Upon yourself – you must be a Narcissus.
Cut your hair short. For if you let it grow
Soon you will see yourself lifted aloft by your hair.

Exit LAURETA.

ABSALOM: Wait a moment! She has gone. If I'm to be
Lifted aloft by my hair, my wish will be granted.
I will succeed in conquering the kingdom.
Lifted aloft by my hair? It must be that Israel
Will somehow be driven crazy by my beauty
And be obliged to offer me the crown.

AMNON: Absalom, you look as mystified as we were.

ABSALOM: Come, princes, let us go in and dine.

Aside.

And soon
I shall be seated on my father's throne.
Amnon will die at the feast, Tamar be avenged
And the way be cleared for Absalom to inherit.

Enter a SERVANT.

SERVANT: The food is getting cold
And begs your Highnesses to come and eat it.

AMNON: I long to see the face of this peasant girl.
Brothers go in and I shall follow you.

ABSALOM: Don't keep us waiting too long.

Aside.

Lifted aloft by my hair, I shall come to reign.

Exeunt omnes except AMNON and TAMAR.

AMNON: Woman, I have an itch to see your eyes.
They must be remarkable, for they have won my soul.
Will you cure this itch of mine?

TAMAR: You'd soon lose interest.
As soon as you had won the first round in the game
You'd want to get up and leave.

AMNON: Your hands are fine.

TAMAR: They are a shepherdess's hands.

AMNON: Let me have one.

TAMAR: It would be fruitless to give my hand to a man
So torn between adoration and abhorrence.

AMNON: Nonetheless I shall take it. Your beauty obliges me.

TAMAR: How will you take it?

AMNON: By force.

TAMAR: You are too fond
Of forcing things.

AMNON: And that's enough of that.
Everyone here seems to have second sight.

TAMAR: You trick us. We're learning how to trick you back.

AMNON: Are you bringing flowers?

TAMAR: Every woman on earth,
Noble or humble, seeks the flower she is lacking.

AMNON: I love you well enough, you little peasant.
Give me a flower.

TAMAR: You have a bunch already.
Believe me, if I had not lost a flower,
I would not feel such sickness as I do.

AMNON: I'll take a flower.

TAMAR: I suppose you mean you'll take
A flower of Tamar.

AMNON: I'll force you. Give it me.

TAMAR: You're fond of forcing, aren't you? Here, take these,
If that is what you want.

She gives him the violets.

AMNON: Violets?

TAMAR: To make you happy

83

> The only flower I can give you, Amnon, is
> A violated one.

AMNON: This is too much for second sight. Unveil yourself.

TAMAR: Let go of me.

AMNON: I'll force that veil off you.

He unveils her.

TAMAR: You are too fond of forcing.

AMNON: Monster, it is you.
> Better put out my eyes than look at you.
> You're an affront to women. I must go.
> I think I shall leave my life here.
> The sight of you has killed something in me.
> I never thought the feast would begin like this.

Exit AMNON.

TAMAR: And the dessert will be worse, you monster.
> The last dish served will be Tamar's revenge.

Exit TAMAR. Enter the shepherds, singing, bearing branches and bouquets.

CHORUS: *Cut the branches from the tree.*
> *Gather the flowers and come with me.*

SOLO: *For Absalom, for Absalom,*
> *Bring poplar, palm and cinnamon.*

CHORUS: *Cut the branches from the tree.*
> *Gather the flowers and come with me.*

SOLO: *For Adonijah let us weave*
> *Carnations and roses finely wreathed.*

CHORUS: *Cut the branches from the tree.*
> *Gather the flowers and come with me.*

SOLO: *For Amnon let us make a crown.*
> *Cut the solemn cypress down.*

CHORUS: *Cut the branches from the tree.*
> *Gather the flowers and come with me.*

SOLO: *Only Solomon is wise.*
   He shall have laurel for his prize.

CHORUS: *Cut the branches from the tree.*
   Gather the flowers and come with me.

Cries within, and sounds of blows, and falling tables and crockery smashing. SOLOMON and ADONIJAH run on, fleeing the scene offstage.

ABSALOM: You will pay for this dinner with your life, you vermin.

AMNON: Brother, why are you attacking me?

ABSALOM: To avenge Tamar.

AMNON: Heaven have mercy. I am done for.

SOLOMON: Run for it.

ADONIJAH: Absalom is an animal. He is lawless.
   All the king's sons live by the sword,
   Die by the sword.

Exeunt SOLOMON and ADONIJAH.

TIRSO: Shit, this is bad.

ARDELIO: Run or we'll be caught in the crossfire.

BRAULIO: What a black gift for a feast.

TIRSO: Absalom eats peacocks.
   I'll stick to my chickens.

ARDELIO: Shut up or they'll have us beheaded.

Exeunt TIRSO, ARDELIO and BRAULIO. Silver sideboards are revealed upon which sits broken crockery which also litters the ground. There is also a table covered with fine food but completely ruined, the linen soaked in blood. AMNON is seated at the table, but lies face up, a cup in one hand and a knife in the other, pierced through the throat with a dagger. ABSALOM and TAMAR enter.

ABSALOM: Sister, this banquet was arranged for you.
   This dish, though foul to eat, has set to rights
   The injustice done to us. Savour it well.

Drink his blood, Tamar. Let it wash away
The stains upon your honour. The bleach is hot.
It will be easy to rinse them out.
Now I must flee to Geshur, our grandfather's kingdom.

TAMAR: And I give thanks to heaven. From this day forth
I shall not weep over this wrong, my valiant brother.
I can look Israel in the face again,
Knowing my honour has been brought back to life.
This blood is like a banner proclaiming my innocence.
Stay there and rot, you animal, you dog.
This tomb, this table set with food and wine,
Is right for sinners like you.

ABSALOM: My hope is now I shall inherit the kingdom.

TAMAR: May heaven grant your wish.

ABSALOM: I have my friends
And, with their help, as the woman said,
Israel shall see me lifted aloft by my hair.

*Exeunt, and the discovery space is covered once more. Enter King
DAVID alone.*

DAVID: Amnon, my son, my prince, if that is you,
My heart is happy,
And every second seems a century.
In spite of all my suspicions and my doubts,
Seeing you here again, thanks be to God,
I have again the life I lose when you
Are gone. How have you been? How are you, son?
Let me embrace your neck, setting a lily
Next to a rose, adorning gold with steel.

He goes to embrace him the empty air.

Give me your arms. O flattering deceptions,
What is this trick, that I embrace the air?
It's like a mother, calming her suckling child,
Dangling a golden jewel, then hiding it,
Or like an illusion at sea, when the black clouds
Appear like distant mountains, promising land.

It's like the stroke of a paintbrush, like a beauty
Seen in a glass, a treasure glimpsed in a dream,
Like the taste of water to a dying man –
Cruel hopes, all of them. Why do you mock me?
And why do you torment my sleepless days?
Where are you, Amnon? Just to see your face
Would make an old man young. It is a sun
And it would melt away the ice of my fears.
Supposing Absalom has taken revenge,
Made you the lamb sacrificed for the feast?
No, in the end Absalom is your brother.
Blood boils. It does not burn. He would not kill him.
And yet, he is of Jacob's line, of the blood
Of one who sold his brother as a slave.
David will weep like Jacob if he finds
That vengeance has killed Amnon.
But Absalom swore not to harm his brother.
Why should I tremble? Those who are in love
And those who have lost their honour never keep
Their promises. My mind is in a whirl
And hope and fear put arguments for and against.
Heaven grant a judgment in my favour now.
I can hear horses. Maybe here come my sons.
Come back, my soul, to my eyes.
Eyes, open to see them well.
Fear has my feet in chains.
Hope flies out to my sons.

Enter ADONIJAH and SOLOMON, with great sadness.

My sons.

ADONIJAH: My Lord.

DAVID: Is everything well with you?
Where are the other two? Will you not speak?
Silence was always the herald of misfortune.
You have been weeping. Too many messengers
Come to confirm my fears. O my prophetic doubt.
Has Absalom killed his brother?

SOLOMON: Yes sir, he has.

DAVID: Then I must lose all hope. I have lost Amnon.
   Let me weep now. Let me weep ever more.
   I have been sentenced to a life of sorrow
   And shall not cease to weep till I am blind.
   Let my tongue speak only in misereres
   And let my ears only hear lamentations.
   Ah, Amnon, ah, my son, my son and heir,
   David your father weeps as Jacob wept
   And says like him: My son, a wild beast has killed you.

ADONIJAH: And here the story of Tamar comes to an end
   In wretched tragedy.

Finis.